# Fantasies & Flowers

*Origami in Fabric for Quilters*

## Making the Block

1. Cut base square of background fabric measuring 15″ × 15″ (38cm × 38cm), including ½″ (1.3cm) seam allowance.
2. Using templates on page 94 and adding ⅛″ (0.3cm) seam allowance, lightly outline pattern onto base.
3. Fold seven prickle pieces B, first vertically then horizontally, as marked on template. Appliqué stems C and D, tucking prickles beneath them as you sew.
4. Appliqué eight leaf pieces A, including four reverse pieces.
5. Appliqué piece E, two pieces F, and six pieces G onto base, taking care to balance them well.

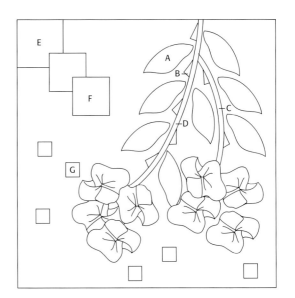

## Making the Flowers

Make 10

1. Place two template H pieces right sides together. Sew around them, leaving opening. Turn right side out. Blind stitch opening closed. Finger press seam.

2. Mark with sewing guide HH on front side of H, and stitch. Pull thread to gather. Vary the tightness of the gathers to vary the shapes of the flowers. Backstitch twice to hold. Attach to base.

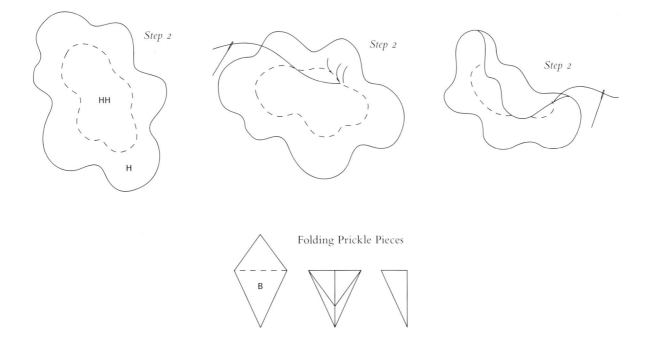

# Wild Begonia Quilt

## Quilt size

34″ × 34″ (86cm × 86cm)

## Block size

14″ × 14″ (36cm × 36cm)

## Border

3″ (7cm)

## Setting

2 × 2

## Blocks

4

## Fabric needed

| Piece | Yards | M |
| --- | --- | --- |
| Background | 1 | 1 |
| A | ¼ | 0.2 |
| B | ⅛ | 0.1 |
| C | ⅛ | 0.1 |
| D | ⅛ | 0.1 |
| E | ⅛ | 0.1 |
| F | ⅛ | 0.1 |
| G | ⅛ | 0.1 |
| H | 1 | 0.1 |
| Border | ½ | 0.5 |
| Batting | 1½ | 1.5 |
| Backing | 1½ | 1.5 |

## Background

15″ × 15″ (38cm × 38cm)

## Cutting

| Piece | Quantity |
| --- | --- |
| Background | 4 |
| A | 28 (12 reverse) |
| B | 28 (12 reverse) |
| C | 4 |
| D | 4 |
| E | 4 |
| F | 8 |
| G | 24 |
| H | 80 |

## Border

Cut 3½″ (8cm) including ¼″ (0.5cm) seam allowance.

Use photograph and diagrams on previous pages as guide to assembly.

# Zinnia Elegans

Every Friday the little opossum was sent by his mother to the store at the end of the village to buy three silver eggs. It was not his favorite errand. One Friday when the opossum was trudging along his weary way, Uncle Mantis stopped him and gave him a tin can. He stuck his long nose inside and found a little silver flower dancing and laughing at him. When the little opossum ran, the zinnia flower ran alongside him. And when he rolled in the grass, it rolled, too. The little opossum was so happy that he forgot himself. He hopped and jumped along the road until he finally arrived at the egg store. He laid the three eggs carefully into his basket. The zinnia helped him carry them home. When they arrived, the little flower promised to see him again the following Friday and disappeared into thin air.

## Making the Block

1. Cut base square of background fabric measuring 15″ × 15″ (38cm × 38cm), including ½″ (1.3cm) seam allowance. Cut piece 2½″ × 15″ (6.4cm × 38cm).
2. Using templates on page 95 and adding ⅛″ (0.3cm) seam allowance, lightly outline pattern onto base.
3. Appliqué three leaves A.
4. Appliqué stem F-1. Appliqué stem D-1 over stem F-1.
5. Appliqué stem E-1. Appliqué stem D-2 over stem E-1.
6. Appliqué stem F-2. Appliqué stem E-2 over stem F-2.
7. Appliqué five leaves B and four leaves C.
8. Make 14 loops K by folding in and stitching the seam allowances. Pin the bottom of each loop in position under L.
9. Appliqué piece L over background fabric and bottoms of loops.

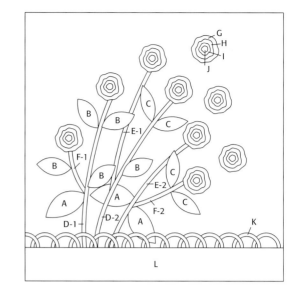

## Making the Flowers

Make 9

Note: This flower is known in quilting as a yo-yo and uses a single circle of fabric rather than the back-to-back fabrics used in other designs in this book.

1. With wrong side of template G facing, fold seam allowance toward you and stitch along folded edge, gathering as you go. At the halfway point, stuff with a little cotton. Gather all the way and backstitch twice to hold.
2. Repeat with templates H, I, and J, without stuffing cotton.
3. Sew H, I, and J onto G. Attach to base.

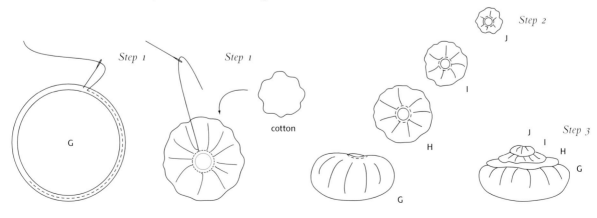

# Foxglove

The north wind blew the powdery snow until it danced in the air. A fox and her pup, cold and hungry after a weary day of fruitless hunting, spied a leafy green foxglove in their path. The fox made a pair of mittens with its leaves for the pup and carried him on her back. Warm and cozy at last, he drifted off to sleep. Safe in their foxhole, the mother curled up with her sleeping son and the two of them slept peacefully for days. One afternoon when the warm sun fell across them, the pup awoke to find the pretty mittens on his hands. He jumped up and found a pile of nuts by the doorway. Foxglove flowers were blooming nearby. Yes, spring had come at last.

## Making the Block

1. Cut base square of background fabric measuring 15″ × 15″ (38cm × 38cm), including ½″ (1.3cm) seam allowance.
2. Using templates on pages 96–97 and adding ⅛″ (0.3cm) seam allowance, lightly outline pattern onto base.
3. Appliqué leaves A to K onto base. Appliqué stems L and M onto base and leaves.

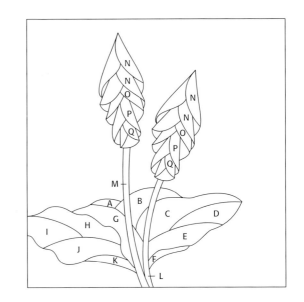

## Making the Flowers

Make 2. Make 4 petals with template N; 2 each with templates O, P, and Q.

1. Place two same-size template pieces right sides together. Sew around them, leaving opening. Turn right side out. Blind stitch opening closed. Finger press seam.
2. Fold petal Q along dotted lines and stitch three times to hold.
3. Position petal Q onto center of P and stitch three times to hold. Fold P along dotted lines and stitch three times to hold, wrapping Q.
4. Repeat, positioning first two petals onto center of O.
5. Repeat, positioning first three petals onto center of N. Repeat, positioning all four petals onto second N piece. Sew completed flower onto base, with three stitches at top and bottom.

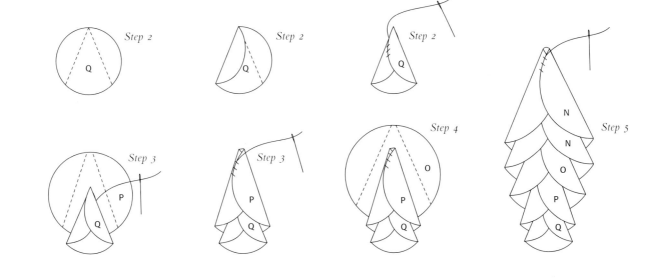

# Azalea

Melony, a monarch butterfly, grew weary gathering nectar. She fell asleep under the shade of a sunflower and dreamed that she was floating effortlessly in the sky. A gust of wind awoke her to the sound of crickets singing in a bush nearby. It was a warm, lazy summer afternoon and Melony felt like flying far away, high above the clouds. She flew and flew until she was too tired to move her wings. She found herself on a beautiful coastal path. As she looked down, she saw wild azalea flowers all along the white sea shore, as far as the eye could see. A vast blue-green ocean rolled into the shore. Melony felt a pleasant ocean breeze on her cheeks. She landed gently on an azalea leaf, closed her tired wings, and fell into a deep sleep, breathing in the flower's fresh fragrance.

## Making the Block

1. Cut base square of background fabric measuring 15″ × 15″ (38cm × 38cm), including ½″ (1.3cm) seam allowance.
2. Using templates on page 98 and adding ⅛″ (0.3cm) seam allowance, lightly outline pattern onto base.
3. Appliqué branches A and B onto base.
4. Appliqué leaves C-1 to C-9 onto base.

## Making the Flowers

Make 9

1. Place two template D pieces right sides together. Sew around them, leaving opening. Turn right side out. Blind stitch opening closed. Finger press seam.
2. Mark center square as shown using template.

3. Fold down point A twice as shown, so that it is 1″ (2.5cm) from top of center square, making a triangle. Pin. Repeat with points B, C, and D.
4. Mark center circle using the template as your guide. Stitch along outer edge of circle. Pull thread and gather. Backstitch twice to hold. Attach onto leaves on base.

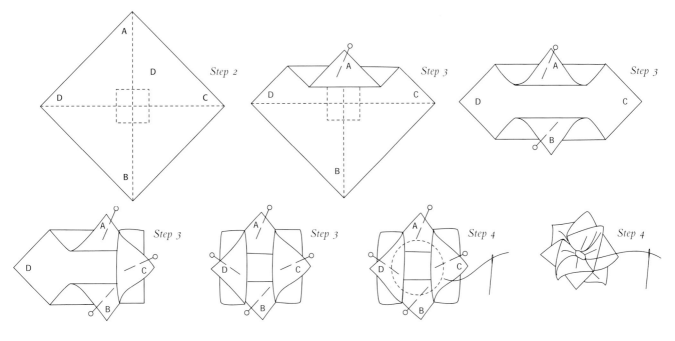

# Campanula

For hundreds of years, a temple stood alone in the middle of a field. At the center of the courtyard grew a lovely flower that the monks took great care to protect. Each April, a festival was held to protect the souls at the temple. On festival day, all the people from the village and all the creatures from the woods and fields gathered together. All paths to the temple were lit by bright lanterns. A young monk picked flowers in the courtyard, filling his bamboo basket. Then he put one flower on each lantern. The flowers moved gently in the soft wind until sunset. As the sun sank, the flowers began to glow faintly and lit the way to the temple, as though they were shining souls. The name of the flower? Yes, it was the campanula.

## Making the Block

1. Cut base square of background fabric measuring 15″ × 15″ (38cm × 38cm), including ½″ (1.3cm) seam allowance.
2. Using templates on page 99 and adding ⅛″ (0.3cm) seam allowance, lightly outline pattern onto base.
3. Appliqué stem pieces A-1 (reverse), A-2, B-1 (reverse), B-2, C-1 (reverse), C-2, D, and E onto base.
4. Appliqué leaf pieces F-1, F-2, F-3, F-4, G-1, and G-2.

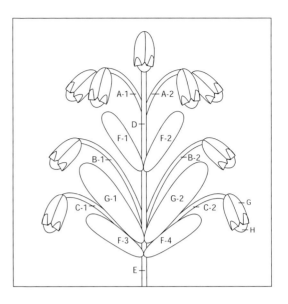

## Making the Flowers

Make 9

1. Place two template H pieces right sides together. Sew around them, leaving opening. Turn right side out. Blind stitch opening closed. Finger press seam.
2. Using the template as your guide, fold three points A of triangle toward center and stitch.
3. Fold along dotted line B-C. Whipstitch along short edge as shown. Turn over. Fold softly along line D-E so that three points A of original triangle meet.
4. With a needle and thread, gather points E together, stitching once through each side and pulling the needle through. Backstitch twice to hold.
5. Put a little amount of cotton in center of I. Stitch around I. Pull thread to gather. Backstitch twice to hold. Sew I onto H as shown. Attach flowers to base.

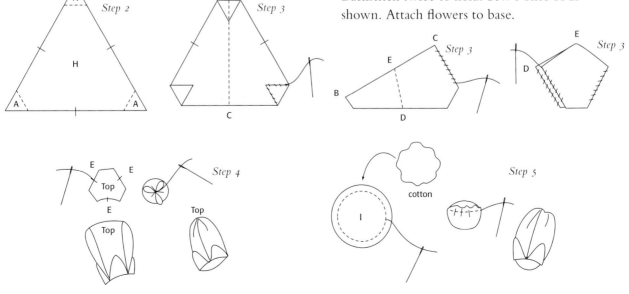

# Bleeding Heart

One summer afternoon, Ritomu, an ant, sat at the top of a camellia. He noticed a stream of bright yellow powder leading into the forest. Curious, Ritomu went to find out where it led, passing cedars and oaks until he reached a great camphor tree. Here, the path stopped. Looking up, he saw a house among the branches and climbed up to peek inside. To his surprise, the ceiling was hung with hearts, and around the room were scattered pieces of broken hearts. A shadow appeared and Ritomu looked up to see a cat with golden hair watching him. The cat asked him if his heart was in need of repair, since it was his job to mend hearts that were broken. He showed Ritomu a beautiful bleeding heart that he was mending. The cat explained that the trail of yellow powder that led to the house was made from the tears of hurting hearts who came for help.

## Making the Block

1. Cut base square of background fabric measuring 15″ × 15″ (38cm × 38cm), including ½″ (1.3cm) seam allowance.
2. Using templates on pages 100–101 and adding ⅛″ (0.3cm) seam allowance, lightly outline pattern onto base.
3. Appliqué stem A onto the background square.
4. Appliqué stem B-1. Appliqué stems C-1 and D-1 in position over stem B-1.
5. Appliqué stem B-2 (reverse) onto base. Appliqué stems C-2 (reverse) and D-2 (reverse) in position over stem B-2.
6. Appliqué leaf E, then leaf F.

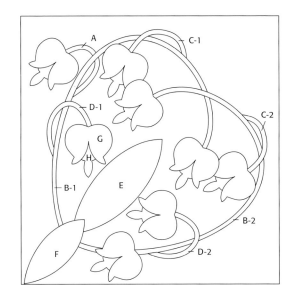

## Making the Flowers

Make 8

1. Place two template G pieces right sides together. Sew around them, leaving an opening from A to B. Make cuts at points A and B and along the curves. Turn right side out.
2. Stitch A to B with small stitches by tucking the seam inside and sewing from the outside.
3. Place two template H pieces right sides together. Sew around them, leaving an opening. Turn right side out. Lightly mark line from template. Stitch along line and gather.
4. Position H inside G and pin to hold.
5. Stitch and gather from C to D.
6. Stitch and gather from A to E and from B to F. Attach completed flowers to base.

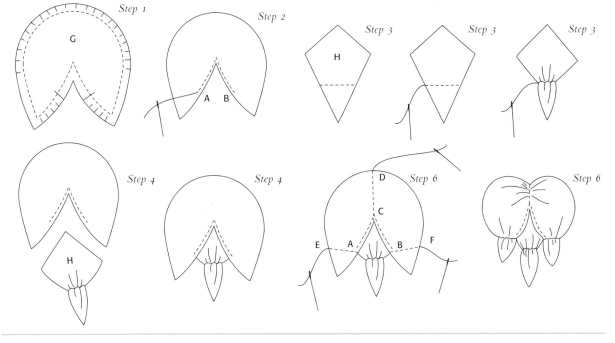

# Bleeding Heart Quilt

## Quilt size

34″ × 34″ (86cm × 86cm)

## Border

3″ (5cm)

## Fabric needed

| Piece | Yards | M |
|---|---|---|
| Background | 1 | 1 |
| A | ⅛ | 0.1 |
| B | ¼ | 0.2 |
| C | ⅛ | 0.1 |
| D | ⅛ | 0.1 |
| E | ⅛ | 0.1 |
| F | ⅛ | 0.1 |
| G | ¾ | 0.7 |
| H | 1 | 0.1 |
| Border | ½ | 0.5 |
| Batting | 1½ | 1.5 |
| Backing | 1½ | 1.5 |

## Background

15″ × 15″ (38cm × 38cm)

## Cutting

| Piece | Quantity |
|---|---|
| Background | 4 |
| A | 4 |
| B | 8 (4 reverse) |
| C | 8 (4 reverse) |
| D | 8 (4 reverse) |
| E | 4 |
| F | 4 |
| G | 64 |
| H | 64 |

## Border

Cut 3½″ (9cm) including ¼″ (0.5cm) seam allowance.

Use photograph and diagrams on previous pages as guide to assembly.

# Phenix

Deep in the forest where nobody had ever walked, there grew Jikajika, the tree of happiness. It bore three kinds of magical fruit. Here lived Florin, a fairy spirit who brightened the lives of the creatures of the forest. Rumors of the tree reached a village, where there lived three old men and three old women. The first couple was always angry, the second couple was always sad, and the third was always irritated. They thought that if only they could see the tree, they could exchange their miserable temperaments for true happiness. For three days, they walked in search of Jikajika. When they saw the tree, they cried out for help. Florin appeared and, seeing how miserable they were, decided to help. She took one of each fruit from the tree and gave one to each couple to eat. Then, in a twinkle of an eye, all six of them smiled, linked arms, and walked happily back to the village.

## Making the Block

1. Cut base square of background fabric measuring 15″ × 15″ (38cm × 38cm), including ½″ (1.3cm) seam allowance.
2. Using templates on pages 101–102 and adding ⅛″ (0.3cm) seam allowance, lightly outline pattern onto base.
3. Appliqué A-1, A-2, and B-2 onto the background square.
4. Appliqué B-1 (reverse) and C-3.
5. Appliqué B-3, C-1, C-2, and D.
6. Appliqué E, F, and G.
7. Appliqué leaves H, I, and J in the following order: I-1, H-1, J-1, I-2, H-2, J-2, H-3, I-3, J-3, I-4, J-4, H-4.
8. Appliqué butterflies K, or butterflies of any size cut from fabric, onto leaves.

## Making the Flowers

Make 5

1. Place two template L pieces right sides together. Sew around them, leaving opening. Turn right side out. Blind stitch opening closed. Finger press seam.

2. Fold A, then B toward C as shown and pin to hold.
3. Fold in half along center line C.
4. Stitch at 1″ (2.5cm) from D toward C and gather. Attach flowers to base.

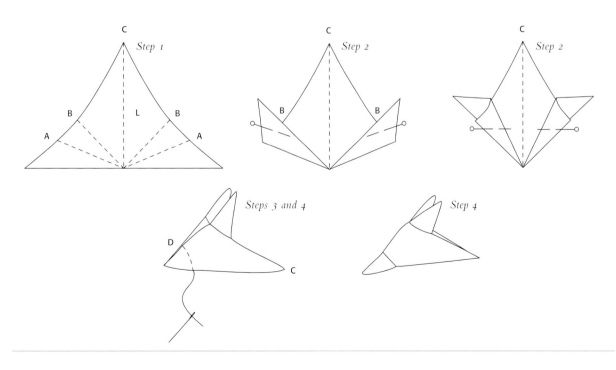

# Hydrangea

One July day, the little ant Ritomu was taking a blueberry pie his mother had baked to his uncle, who owned an apple orchard. On the way, he met Lulu, a dove, who, oddly enough, was delivering a strawberry pie to her aunt. They strolled along together for a while, then, when their paths parted, waved good-bye. Arriving at his uncle's house, Ritomu went into the orchard and happily ran to the very end of the rows of ripening apple trees. To his surprise, there he saw Lulu, who was flying over her aunt's cornfield. Where the cornfield and the orchard met there bloomed dozens of bright hydrangea flowers. Delighted, the two gathered as many of the lovely flowers as they could carry and took them home, where a blueberry pie and a strawberry pie were waiting for them on a table.

## Making the Block

1. Cut base square of background fabric measuring 15″ × 15″ (38cm × 38cm), including ½″ (1.3cm) seam allowance.
2. Using templates on pages 103–105 and adding ⅛″ (0.3cm) seam allowance, lightly outline pattern onto base.
3. Appliqué piece A onto base. Appliqué piece B. Appliqué pieces C and D.
4. Appliqué stems E, F, G, and H.
5. Appliqué pieces I, J, K, and L to make the first leaf; M, N, O, and P to make the second; and Q, R, S, and T to make the third.

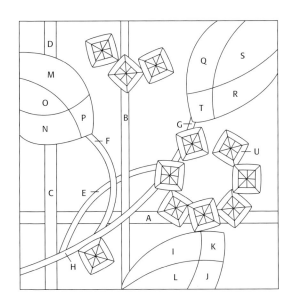

## Making the Flowers

Make 11

1. Place two template U pieces right sides together. Sew around them, leaving opening. Turn right side out. Blind stitch opening closed. Finger press seam.

2. Fold A toward center until it meets center square, roll under as shown, then pin and sew. Repeat with all four corners.
3. Stitch along center circle and pull the thread to gather. Attach flowers to base.

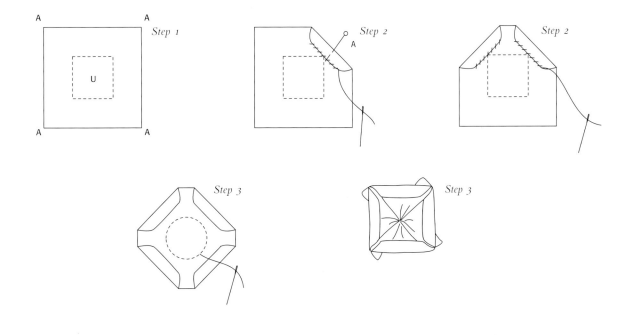

# Gladiolus

Ritomu the ant and his sister, Lilika, were walking in the forest in search of something sweet to eat. To their surprise, they bumped right into the strangest thing they had ever seen—a grand piano! Pleased and excited, they climbed up onto the keys and jumped up and down as wildly as they could to make the piano play. Try as they might, they couldn't make a sound. Then, out of nowhere, dozens of tiny fairies, all in yellow hats, appeared. Quick as the wind, they flitted around the piano. Then, from the tree above, a cherry blossom fell onto one of the keys, playing a soft, sweet note. More and more flowers fell, creating heavenly melodies on the piano keys. Soft among the grasses, the petunia flower joined in and merrily blew her trumpet. The flute of the gladiolus swayed gently to the music, and all the flowers of the forest gathered around the piano. Ritomu and Lilika forgot all about the sweets they had craved and danced until sunset.

## Making the Block

1. Cut base square of background fabric measuring 15″ × 15″ (38cm × 38cm), including ½″ (1.3cm) seam allowance.
2. Using templates on pages 106–107 and adding ⅛″ (0.3cm) seam allowance, lightly outline pattern onto base.
3. Appliqué stem pieces A and B onto base.
4. Appliqué leaf pieces C-2 and D-1 (reverse).
5. Appliqué leaves D-2 and E-1 at the same time, overlapping as necessary. Do the same with leaves C-1 and D-3 (reverse).
6. Appliqué leaf E-2.

## Making the Flowers

Make 10

1. Place two template F pieces right sides together. Sew around them, leaving opening. Turn right side out. Blind stitch opening closed. Finger press seam.
2. Fold in ½″ (1.25cm) at A and C and pin.
3. Fold B diagonally at about 2″ (5cm) and pin.
4. Roll C over A and B.
5. Fold D diagonally as shown and sew both sides. Arrange and attach flowers onto base. If desired, fold some flowers in the opposite direction.

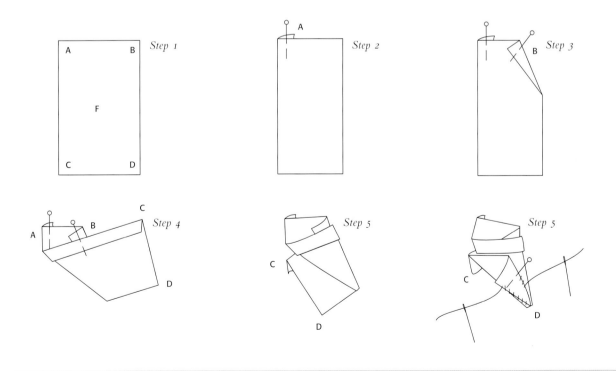

43

# Snapdragon

ika and his mother were gathering leaves to make new whistles when Kika spotted
something glittering gold at the edge of the brook. It was a young snapdragon,
sparkling in the sun. Kika touched it gently, trying to pop the seed, but his mother
hurried him along. Kika saw more of the beautiful flowers, ready to bud. He knew that if he
could just touch their light green bells, the seeds would pop. He sighed and turned to fill his
basket. Before long, he felt his mother's hand on his head. "Good job, Kika," she gently said.
Crossing the brook on the way home, Kika gazed longingly at the wonderful golden
snapdragon. To his delight, his mother touched one of the bells. Out popped the seeds in the
fading sunlight. As they floated away downstream, Kika thought he heard music.
Perhaps it was a fairy's harp, greeting the first flowers of spring.

## Making the Block

1. Cut base square of background fabric measuring 15″ × 15″ (38cm × 38cm), including ½″ (1.3cm) seam allowance.
2. Using templates on pages 107–108 and adding ⅛″ (0.3cm) seam allowance, lightly outline pattern onto base.
3. Appliqué leaves A-1 to A-9 onto base.
4. Appliqué stem B. Appliqué leaf A-10 over stem B.
5. Appliqué leaves A-11 to A-14 onto base.
6. Appliqué stem C. Appliqué leaves A-15 and A-16 over stem C.

## Making the Flowers

Make 9

1. Place two template D pieces right sides together. Sew around them, leaving opening. Turn right side out. Blind stitch opening closed. Finger press seam.
2. Using the template as a guide, fold and pin as shown.
3. Stitch center part and gather.
4. Pull A over B as shown to make flower. Sew onto background square.

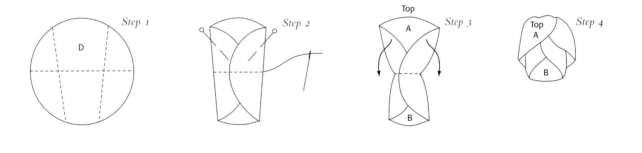

## Making the Seeds

Make 10

1. Sew and gather ten E pieces, as shown. Arrange and sew onto background square.

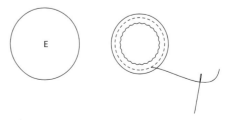

# Periwinkle

High above the oak hills at the point where two mountain streams met, there lived a mysterious boy. It was said that he had the power to heal withered trees and shrubs and bring them back into flower. One bright morning, Lulu, a little dove, and Kurori, a robin, set off to see how this could be so. They found a little house cut from the mountain rocks. A silver tree, bare of leaves or flowers, hung over the house. Lulu and Kurori knocked gingerly on the door. A beautiful boy, with eyes as bright as moonlight, answered, and the two birds explained why they had come. The boy showed them a withered tree that he had found. He told them that at nightfall he would place it among the branches of the silver tree that grew outside. He would then catch a shooting star and hang it from the withered tree. By dawn, the tree would be full of flowers. That night Lulu and Kurori slept outside the house. In the early morning, the sun shone on a beautiful periwinkle tree in full bloom.

## Making the Block

1. Cut base square of background fabric measuring 15″ × 15″ (38cm × 38cm), including ½″ (1.3cm) seam allowance.
2. Using templates on pages 110–112 and adding ⅛″ (0.3cm) seam allowance, lightly outline pattern onto base.
3. Appliqué two pieces A and piece B onto base. Appliqué pieces C and D.
4. Appliqué leaf pieces E, F, and G.
5. Appliqué pieces H and I onto piece J. Appliqué pieces K and L onto M. Appliqué pieces N and O on either side.
6. Appliqué two P pieces onto two Q pieces. Appliqué one of these pieces onto C and the other onto D. Appliqué pieces R and S in place.
7. Appliqué two stems T (one reverse) onto base.
8. Appliqué two leaves U (one reverse) onto stems T. Appliqué two leaves V (one reverse) onto leaves U.

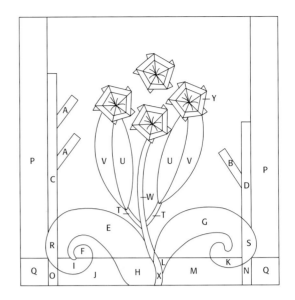

9. Appliqué piece W in place onto stems T. Appliqué piece X.

## Making the Flowers

Make 4

1. Place two template Y pieces right sides together. Sew around them, leaving opening. Turn right side out. Blind stitch opening closed. Finger press seam.
2. Using the template as a guide, roll points A through E inward as shown. Stitch to hold.

3. Draw a 1″ (2.5cm) circle in the center. Stitch along circle, pull thread to gather, and backstitch twice to hold.
4. Tuck five corners to form five petals of flower. Attach to base.

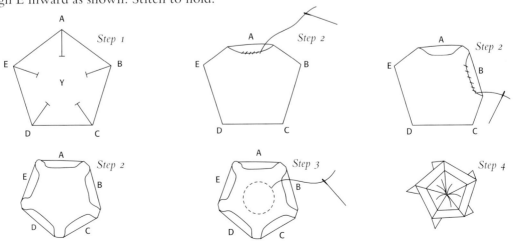

# Periwinkle Quilt

## Quilt size

32″ × 32″ (81cm × 81cm)

## Block size

14″ × 14″ (36cm × 36cm)

## Border

2″ (5cm)

## Setting

2 × 2

## Blocks

4

## Fabric needed

| Piece | Yards | M |
|---|---|---|
| Background | 1 | 1 |
| EE | ⅛ | 0.1 |
| GG | ⅛ | 0.1 |
| HH | ⅛ | 0.1 |
| II | ⅛ | 0.1 |
| KK | ⅛ | 0.1 |
| Q | ⅛ | 0.1 |
| T | ⅛ | 0.1 |
| U | ⅛ | 0.1 |
| V | ⅛ | 0.1 |
| WW | ⅛ | 0.1 |
| Y | ¾ | 0.7 |
| Border rectangles | ½ | 0.5 |
| Corner squares | ⅛ | 0.1 |
| Batting | 1¼ | 1.2 |
| Backing | 1¼ | 1.2 |

## Background

15″ × 15″ (38cm × 38cm)

## Cutting

| Piece | Quantity |
|---|---|
| Background | 4 |
| EE | 4 |
| GG | 4 |
| HH | 4 |
| II | 4 |
| KK | 4 |
| Q | 8 |
| T | 8 (4 reverse) |
| U | 8 (4 reverse) |
| V | 8 (4 reverse) |
| WW | 4 |
| Y | 32 |
| Border rectangles | 24 |
| Corner squares | 4 |

## Border

Cut 24 border rectangles 2½″ × 5″ (5cm × 11.4cm). Cut four corner squares 2½″ × 2½″ (6cm × 6cm).

Use photograph and diagrams on previous pages as guide to assembly.

Note: The additional templates for this quilt are on page 109.

# Coral Tree

There was a rugged road over a green hill, leading to the spot where a coral tree grew. Melony, a butterfly, came to rest on the grass at the bottom of the hill. She saw a turtle crawling toward her, wheezing with every step. When he finally reached her, the turtle asked for the place where the coral tree grew. Melony flitted onto the turtle's back and helped him find the way up the hill. As they went, the turtle told Melony that when he was young he lived on a coral reef that had broken apart years before. Pieces of it had scattered around the world, and the turtle had spent his life in search of them. As they reached the hilltop, they saw before them a magnificent coral tree, its red and orange blossoms brilliant against the sky.

## Making the Block

1. Cut base square of background fabric measuring 15″ × 15″ (38cm × 38cm), including ½″ (1.3cm) seam allowance.
2. Using templates on pages 112–114 and adding ⅛″ (0.3cm) seam allowance, lightly outline pattern onto base.
3. Appliqué leaf pieces A to J in alphabetical order. Appliqué leaf pieces K-1 and K-2.
4. Appliqué stem L.
5. To make fence, appliqué pieces O to T in alphabetical order. Appliqué pieces U and V over them.
6. Appliqué leaves M and N. Appliqué leaf W onto M and N.
7. Appliqué stem X onto leaf W. Tuck end of stem under leaf G.

## Making the Flowers

Make 9

1. Place two template Y pieces right sides together. Sew around them, leaving opening. Turn right side out. Blind stitch opening closed. Finger press seam.

2. Fold as shown, leaving about ⅜″ (1cm) of lower fabric uncovered. Stitch and gather.
3. Stitch twice to hold together, as shown. Attach to base.

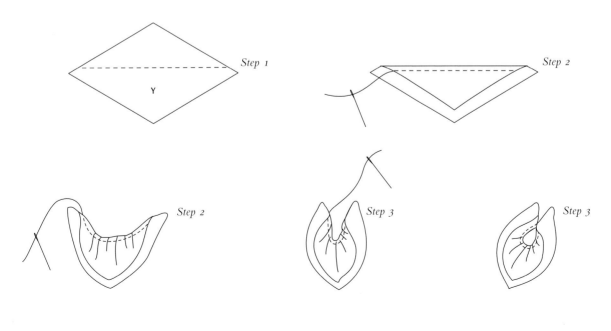

*Step 1*

*Step 2*

*Step 2*

*Step 3*

*Step 3*

# Weeping Cherry

Spending all his savings from eleven long years, Ritomu ordered eleven cherry trees from a nursery on the outskirts of town. Late in the afternoon, the trees were delivered. Hundreds of blossoms danced happily in the spring breeze, shining in seven colors in Ritomu's sunset garden. Later that evening, the creatures of the forest came to rest under Ritomu's cherry trees. They smelled the sweet nectar and slept beneath the spreading leaves. When Ritomu went down to the trees early next morning, he was pleased to see these creatures enjoying their new home. He began to plan the trees he would buy when his savings grew again.

## Making the Block

1. Cut base square of background fabric measuring 15″ × 15″ (38cm × 38cm), including ½″ (1.3cm) seam allowance.
2. Using templates on pages 115–116 and adding ⅛″ (0.3cm) seam allowance, lightly outline pattern onto base.
3. Appliqué cloud pieces A and B onto base.
4. Appliqué trunk C.
5. Appliqué twenty-two D pieces, including six reverse, onto base.

## Making the Flowers

Make 10

1. Place two template E pieces right sides together. Sew around them, leaving opening. Turn right side out. Blind stitch opening closed. Finger press seam.
2. Using the template as a guide, fold up bottom of triangle E and pin.
3. Fold in right side as shown and pin.
4. Fold in left side as shown and pin.
5. Sew four stitches across the bottom, ¾″ (2cm) from the tip. Gather and backstitch to hold. Attach flowers to base. *Note:* Here, I wrapped from right to left. If desired, wrap from left to right.

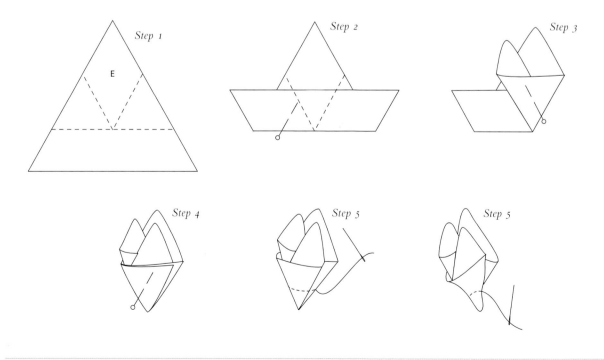

# Winter Daphne

F ebruary passed in a blink of an eye and new buds appeared on the trees and shrubs. But on Flower Hill, where the lizard family lived, there were no signs of spring at all. The lizards were sad, as they had spent the long winter days dreaming of fragrant flowers on a colorful hillside. The father lizard decided he must do something to save the hill. He went to his friend the honeybee and told him of his plight. The kind honeybee gave the lizard five special kinds of pollen, telling him to mix them carefully and spread the mixture on the ground. The lizard worked late into the night, making sure that every tree and shrub on the hillside received some of the precious pollen. After a week, the hill was alive with color and fragrance. The flowers chattered to each other and greeted the spring. Happiest of all was the honeybee, who buzzed from flower to flower tasting their sweet nectar.

## Making the Block

1. Cut base square of background fabric measuring 15″ × 15″ (38cm × 38cm), including ½″ (1.3cm) seam allowance.
2. Using templates on page 117 and adding ⅛″ (0.3cm) seam allowance, lightly outline pattern onto base.
3. Appliqué five stems A onto background square.
4. Place two leaf B pieces right sides together, leaving an opening. Turn right side out. Blind stitch opening closed. Finger press seam. Repeat four times, for a total of five leaf pieces.
5. Fold each leaf piece as shown or as desired and sew onto base.

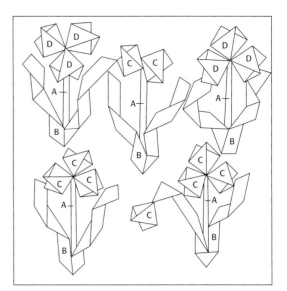

## Making the Flowers

Make 9 small flowers with template C and 6 large flowers with template D

1. Place two pieces cut with the same template right sides together. Sew around them, leaving opening. Turn right side out. Blind stitch opening closed. Finger press seam.
2. Fold A back toward B, overlapping as shown.
3. Fold C toward B, reverse overlapping as shown. Attach to base.

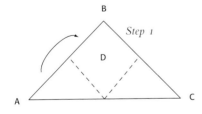

*Step 1*

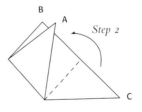

*Step 2*

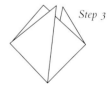

*Step 3*

# Crown Imperial

In early March, with the call of a spring breeze, Momo, a baby mole, peeked out from his tunnel into a green field. The plum flowers were abloom, their fragrance filling the air, and the cherry trees swelled with buds. Excited to be outside in the fresh, crisp air, Momo forgot all his mother had taught him and ran mischievously into a nearby garden. There, he saw a small boy playing with bright balloons in the sunshine and ran to join in the fun. Seeing him, the boy let go of his balloons and chased the baby mole. Frightened, his heart beating fast, Momo ran for cover and hid in a tiny hole in a big oak tree. Safe in his hiding place, he watched as the balloons floated away in the wind past a hillside that was ablaze with bright crown imperial flowers. He snuggled down to sleep and dreamed of the flowers, playing in the spring breeze.

## Making the Block

1. Cut base square of background fabric measuring 15″ × 15″ (38cm × 38cm), including ½″ (1.3cm) seam allowance.
2. Using templates on pages 117–118 and adding ⅛″ (0.3cm) seam allowance, lightly outline pattern onto base.
3. Appliqué heart I and two hearts J onto base. Draw the strings and embroider as desired.
4. Appliqué drape pieces E, F, G, and H.
5. Appliqué stem A and leaves B-1, B-2, and C-1.
6. Appliqué leaf B-3, stem D, and leaves B-4 and C-2 in that order.
7. Appliqué flower pieces K to P in alphabetical order. Repeat for second flower.

## Making the Flowers

Make 6

1. Place two template Q pieces right sides together. Sew around them, leaving opening. Turn right side out. Blind stitch opening closed. Finger press seam.

2. Fold hexagon across center line A.
3. Fold point C inward to point D as shown, making an inverted fold on each side. Repeat on other side. Pin and sew as shown. Attach to base.

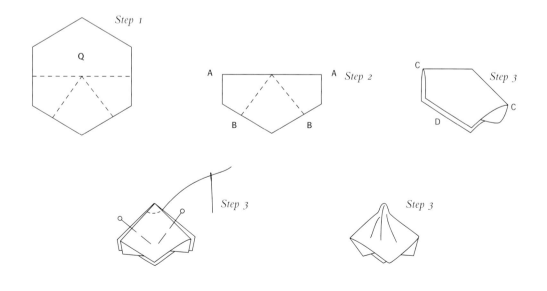

# Snow Pea

A snow pea family lived in the garden of Aunt Mizet, who took good care of them. Whenever they put out shoots, she would plant a bamboo shoot alongside them to help them grow straight up to the sky. Aunt Mizet loved to tell stories, for she believed that they would help her flowers grow. The story that the snow peas loved the best was about a village that floated way up above the sky. In this magical village there was a restaurant that was built of strawberries. There, squirrel waiters with silver wings served delicious meals, while the clouds played the most wondrous melodies. Under Aunt Mizet's window, the snow peas listened. They couldn't wait for the summer, when up they would sprout, high into the sky.

## Making the Block

1. Cut base square of background fabric measuring 15″ × 15″ (38 cm × 38 cm), including ½″ (1.3 cm) seam allowance.
2. Using templates on pages 119–120 and adding ⅛″ (0.3 cm) seam allowance, lightly outline pattern onto base.
3. Appliqué stem pieces A to J in alphabetical order.
4. Appliqué leaf pieces K and L onto stems as follows: K-1, K-2, K-3, K-4, K-5, K-6, L-1, K-7, L-2, L-3, L-4, L-5, L-6, L-7, L-8.

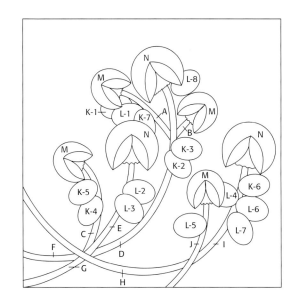

## Making the Flowers

Make 3 small flowers with template M and 3 large flowers with template N

1. Place two pieces cut with the same template right sides together. Sew around them, leaving opening. Turn right side out. Blind stitch opening closed. Finger press seam.

2. Using the template as a guide, sew across as shown. Pull thread to gather. Fold bottom piece back and stitch in place along same stitch line.
3. Fold A to B as shown.
4. Fold both sides C toward center. Stitch two or three times at point D to hold. Attach flowers to base.

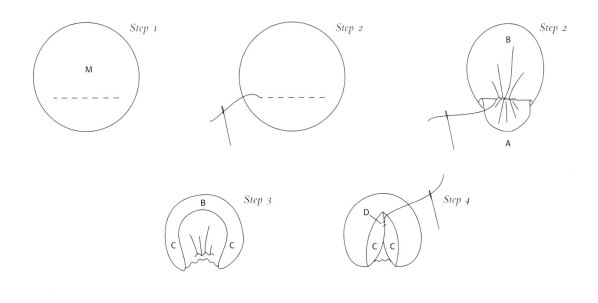

# Snow Pea Quilt

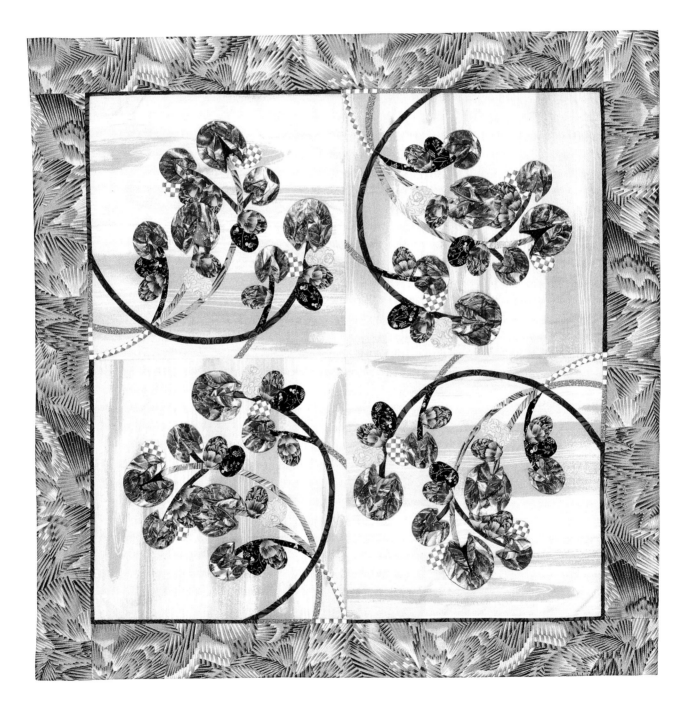

## Quilt size

34″ × 34″ (86cm × 86cm)

## Block size

14″ × 14″ (36cm × 36cm)

## Border

3″ (7cm)

## Setting

2 × 2

## Blocks

4

## Fabric needed

| Piece | Yards | M |
| --- | --- | --- |
| Background | 1 | 1 |
| A | ⅛ | 0.1 |
| B | ⅛ | 0.1 |
| C | ⅛ | 0.1 |
| D | ⅛ | 0.1 |
| E | ⅛ | 0.1 |
| F | ⅛ | 0.1 |
| G | ⅛ | 0.1 |
| H | ⅛ | 0.1 |
| I | ⅛ | 0.1 |
| J | ⅛ | 0.1 |
| K | ¼ | 0.2 |
| L | ¼ | 0.2 |
| M | ¼ | 0.2 |
| N | ¼ | 0.2 |
| Border | ½ | 0.5 |
| Piping | 3¼ | 3.2 |
| Batting | 1½ | 1.5 |
| Backing | 1½ | 1.5 |

## Background

15″ × 15″ (38cm × 38cm)

## Piping (optional)

¼″ (0.5cm)

## Cutting

| Piece | Quantity |
| --- | --- |
| A | 4 |
| B | 4 |
| C | 4 |
| D | 4 |
| E | 4 |
| F | 4 |
| G | 4 |
| H | 4 |
| I | 4 |
| J | 4 |
| K | 28 |
| L | 32 |
| M | 24 |
| N | 24 |

## Border

Cut 3½″ (8cm) including ¼″ (0.5cm) seam allowance.

Use photograph and diagrams on previous pages as guide to assembly.

# Apple Tree

Every year, ripe apples were sent to the city from the apple orchards up north. On one farm there was a huge tree that had not borne fruit for many seasons. There was talk about cutting it down, but just in time the tree bore the biggest, most beautiful apple ever seen. It smelled so wonderful that Taro, a caterpillar, climbed up the tree to take just one taste. To his surprise, the apple whispered, "Please, little caterpillar, take one of the seeds from my heart and carry it to the city so that it can be with the apples that are sent there each year. I have been so lonely." A tear dropped onto Taro's shoulder. Taro took one of the precious seeds and carried it all the way to the city, where he planted it in the middle of the park. Three years passed before Taro returned. There before him was a lovely blossoming apple tree. Taro crept onto one of its branches, fresh with morning dew, and nestled down to sleep.

## Making the Block

1. Cut base square of background fabric measuring 15″ × 15″ (38cm × 38cm), including ½″ (1.3cm) seam allowance.
2. Using templates on pages 120–122 and adding ⅛″ (0.3cm) seam allowance, lightly outline pattern onto base.
3. Appliqué leaf pieces A-1, A-2, B-1, B-2, and B-3 onto the base.
4. Appliqué pieces E and F onto C and D.
5. Appliqué B-4, B-5, and A-3.
6. Appliqué six small branch pieces G, then one large branch piece H.
7. Appliqué trunk pieces I, J, and K. Then appliqué trees L, M, and N on top of the trunks.
8. Appliqué pieces O, P, and Q.

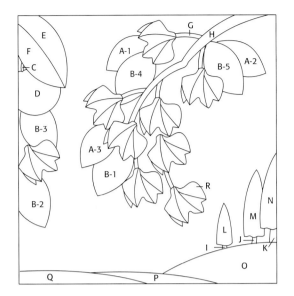

## Making the Flowers

Make 8

1. Place two template R pieces right sides together. Sew around them, leaving opening. Turn right side out. Blind stitch opening closed. Finger press seam.
2. Match B to B, right sides together, then pin at center. Stitch twice to hold. Match A to A, reverse sides together, then pin at center. Stitch twice to hold.
3. Mark the center circle using template S. Sew and gather to complete flower. Attach to base. *Note:* Try changing the shape of the flowers by manipulating the fabric gently with your fingers.

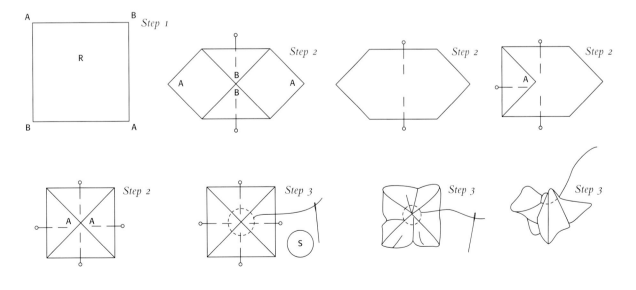

# Crepe Myrtle

Pelulu, a dove, lived happily in the forest with her seven children. One day she noticed that Lulu, her youngest, didn't often play with the others and seemed to spend too much time alone, sitting quietly high up in the tree. She called her other children together and asked them to think up a special treat for Lulu to cheer her. They knew that Lulu liked above all else to play with pretty papers, so they decided to find some for her. Early the next morning they flew to a nearby village and plucked tiny scraps of ribbons and papers from market stalls, from open windows, and wherever they found them. They collected everything together in a wicker basket, tied with a green bow. Carefully, they placed it next to Lulu where she slept. Delighted, Lulu awoke to see her gift and began to make all kinds of things. She shaped some pieces into nuts and decorated a withered tree with them. The next morning, the nuts had magically changed into delicious red fruits, which she shared with her brothers and sisters.

## Making the Block

1. Cut base square of background fabric measuring 15″ × 15″ (38cm × 38cm), including ½″ (1.3cm) seam allowance.
2. Using templates on pages 123–124 and adding ⅛″ (0.3cm) seam allowance, lightly outline pattern onto base.
3. Appliqué stem pieces A-1 to A-5. (A-3 is reversed.)
4. Appliqué D onto stems A-1 and A-2. Appliqué B-1 onto stems A-4 and A-5. Appliqué stem pieces B-2 (reverse) and C.
5. Appliqué three leaf pieces E at the right side.
6. Appliqué center stem piece F.
7. Appliqué five leaf pieces E at the left side and appliqué stem piece G onto them.

## Making the Flowers

Make 26

1. Place two template H pieces right sides together. Sew around them, leaving opening. Turn right side out. Blind stitch opening closed. Finger press seam.

2. Stitch as shown, using the template as a guide. Stuff center with cotton and gather to close. Backstitch to hold. Attach to base.

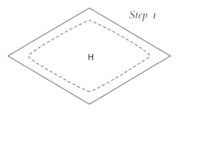

*Step 1*

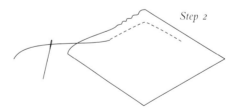

*Step 2*

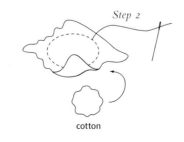

*Step 2*

cotton

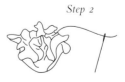

*Step 2*

# Evening Primrose

The creatures of the field were planning a midnight party. Kusukusu the snail, dressed in his black mantle, was in charge. The ants, mice, spiders, and moles all chattered excitedly. Kusukusu heard sobs and turned to see three flower buds, their eyes streaming with tears. When Kusukusu asked why, they stammered that they thought no one would want them at the party because their faces were too sharp. Kusukusu laughed gently and told them not to worry. He explained that the summer night would transform them. "Look at the moon," he said. "See how she changes from night to night. Sometimes she is just a slither, and other times we see her full face; yet she is always beautiful. You, too, can change." As the sun sank and a dark blue sky covered the heavens, the three buds looked up to see the big round face of the moon. Softly, their flowers opened, round and full, as though to imitate the moon.

The evening primroses were blooming and the midnight party began.

## Making the Block

1. To create base, cut piece A, measuring 3″ × 15″ (7.5cm × 38cm); piece B, measuring 11½″ × 15″ (29.2cm × 38cm); and strip C, measuring ¾″ × 15″ (1.9cm × 38cm). Appliqué strip C onto A. Using templates on pages 124–125 and adding ⅛″ (0.3cm) seam allowance, sew pieces D, E, and F together and appliqué piece onto other side of strip C. Sew this piece to B to complete base.

2. Using templates on pages 124–125 and adding ⅛″ (0.3cm) seam allowance, lightly outline pattern onto base.

3. Appliqué stem and leaf pieces in following order: stem pieces G and H, leaf piece Q, stem pieces I-1 and I-2, leaf pieces M-1 and M-2, stem pieces J, K, and L, and leaf piece M-3.

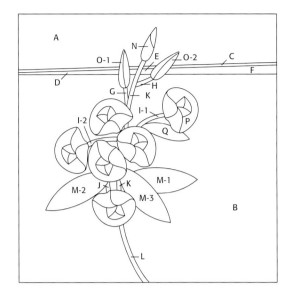

## Making the Buds

Make 2 from template N, 1 from template O

1. Note that templates N and O include seam allowances. Fold along dotted lines. Tuck in and fold at ⅛″ (0.5cm). Sew buds onto stems.

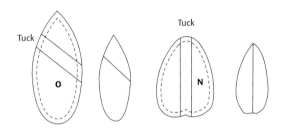

## Making the Flowers

Make 6

1. Place two template P pieces right sides together. Sew around them, leaving opening. Turn right side out. Blind stitch opening closed. Finger press seam.

2. Fold in thirds as shown. Sew along dotted line; gather. Backstitch to hold.

3. Fold B over A.

4. Sew and gather C through all layers to complete flower. Attach to base.

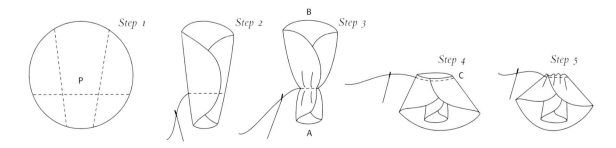

*Step 1*   *Step 2*   *Step 3*   *Step 4*   *Step 5*

# Bougainvillea

Toruton was a kindly magician. Born and raised in Arabia, he had traveled the world over. He came to a village where no one knew of his art. Nearby lived an old woman. Toruton saw her almost every day, but whenever he greeted her, she ignored him.

One rainy day, her horse got stuck in a mud bank. In panic, he reared on his hind legs, frightening his owner out of her wits. Toruton picked up two leaves, cast a spell, and threw them to the horse. Magically, the leaves turned into wings and the horse flew up, freeing himself from the mud. From that day on, the woman was kind to Toruton and baked him blueberry pies.

When winter came, Toruton came across an old man whose cow was stuck in the snow, shivering with cold. Toruton took from his pocket a brilliant red butterfly and tossed it into the sky. Very quickly the air warmed, the snow melted, and bright red blossoms shaped liked butterflies budded on the trees. In surprise, the man led his cow home. Each day he brought Toruton a pitcher of fresh milk. With blueberry pie, delicious milk, and a warm fireplace, the magician gave up his travels and made the village his home.

## Making the Block

1. Cut base square of background fabric measuring 15″ × 15″ (38cm × 38cm), including ½″ (1.3cm) seam allowance.
2. Using templates on pages 126–127 and adding ⅛″ (0.3cm) seam allowance, lightly outline pattern onto base.
3. Appliqué stem pieces A, B, C, D, E, and F.
4. Appliqué leaf piece G-1.
5. Appliqué birds H and I.
6. Appliqué remaining leaf pieces G.

## Making the Flowers

Make 7

1. Place two template J pieces right sides together. Sew around them, leaving opening. Turn right side out. Blind stitch opening closed. Finger press seam.
2. Fold along dotted line as shown.
3. Fold in both sides toward point B.
4. Sew at ½″ (1.25cm) from base, gather, and backstitch to hold. Make petals by pulling the flower apart gently at both sides. Attach to base.

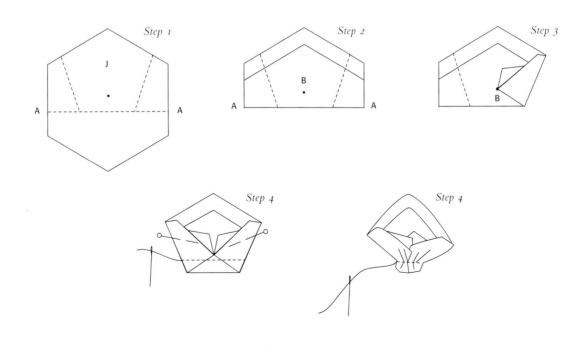

# Daffodil

A child looked up at the moon and asked, "Where did you come from?" The moon looked down on her and answered, "I was born in a land of golden skies, pink clouds, and purple air. To celebrate my birth, the sky gave me a glass full of jam. The clouds made cotton candy for me. The air gave me perfume in a crystal jar. I took these gifts to the hills, where I slept for three days. When I awoke, my face was golden and my cheeks were pink." As the moon talked to the girl, a blue cloud came by and covered half its face. The north wind blew, fluttering among the hundreds of daffodils that grew in the girl's garden. The flowers seemed to laugh with pleasure. The girl brought her face close to them and breathed in their the sweet fragrance. She picked a daffodil. From its stem, she thought she saw a stream of jam. She looked up at the moon and smiled.

## Making the Block

1. Cut base square of background fabric measuring 15″ × 15″ (38cm × 38cm), including ½″ (1.3cm) seam allowance.
2. Using templates on pages 129–131 and adding ⅛″ (0.3cm) seam allowance, lightly outline pattern onto base.
3. Appliqué stem pieces A, B, and C onto base.
4. Appliqué three leaf pieces D, including one reverse, onto base.
5. Appliqué E and F onto base.

## Making the Flowers

Make 2 flowers from template G and 3 flowers from template H

1. Place two pieces cut from the same template right sides together. Sew around them, leaving opening. Turn right side out. Blind stitch opening closed. Finger press seam.

2. Turn under seams of piece I. Blind stitch to center of flower piece as shown.
3. Make a circle of stitches on flower piece, ⅛″ (0.3cm) from perimeter of I. Gather and backstitch to hold. Attach to base.

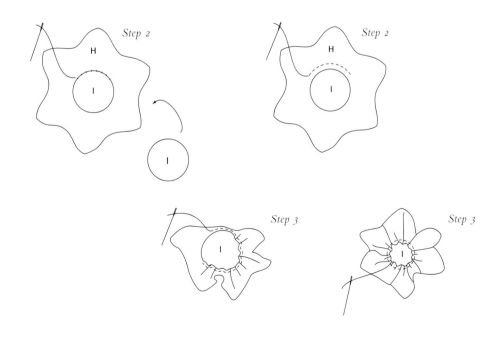

# Daffodil Quilt

## Quilt size

32″ × 45″ (81cm × 114cm)

## Block size

7″ × 7″ (18cm × 18cm)

## Borders

1½″ (3.8cm)
2″ (5cm)

## Setting

4 × 6

## Blocks

24

## Fabric needed

| Piece | Yards | M |
| --- | --- | --- |
| Background | 1½ | 1.5 |
| AA | ¼ | 0.2 |
| BB | ¼ | 0.2 |
| CC | ¼ | 0.2 |
| DD | ¼ | 0.2 |
| H | 1¼ | 1.2 |
| Top border | ⅛ | 0.1 |
| Side border | ⅜ | 0.3 |
| Batting | 1½ | 1.5 |
| Backing | 1½ | 1.5 |

## Background

8″ × 8″ (20cm × 20cm)

## Cutting

| Piece | Quantity |
| --- | --- |
| Background | 24 |
| AA | 16 (reverse 8) |
| BB | 12 (reverse 6) |
| CC | 16 (reverse 8) |
| DD | 24 (reverse 12) |
| H | 48 |

## Border

Cut 2″ (4.8cm) and 2½″ (6cm) borders including ¼″ (0.5cm) seam allowance.

Use photograph and diagrams on previous pages as guide to assembly.

Note: The additional templates for this quilt are on page 128.

# Templates

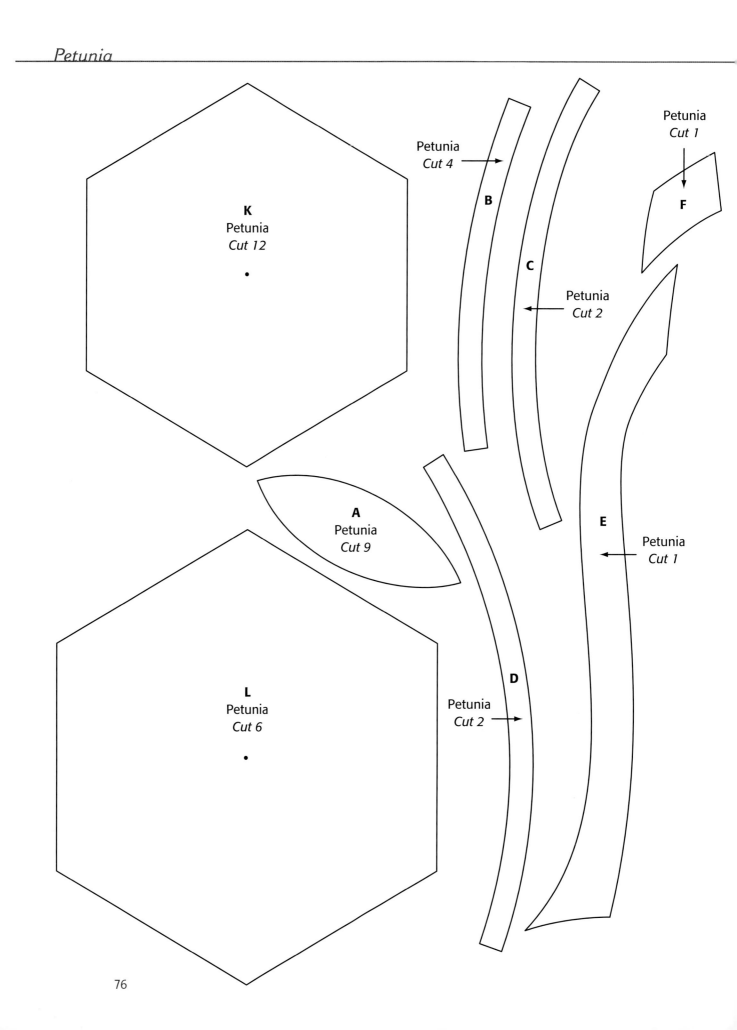

**K**
Petunia
*Cut 12*

Petunia
*Cut 4*

**B**

**C**

Petunia
*Cut 2*

Petunia
*Cut 1*

**F**

**A**
Petunia
*Cut 9*

**E**

Petunia
*Cut 1*

**L**
Petunia
*Cut 6*

**D**

Petunia
*Cut 2*

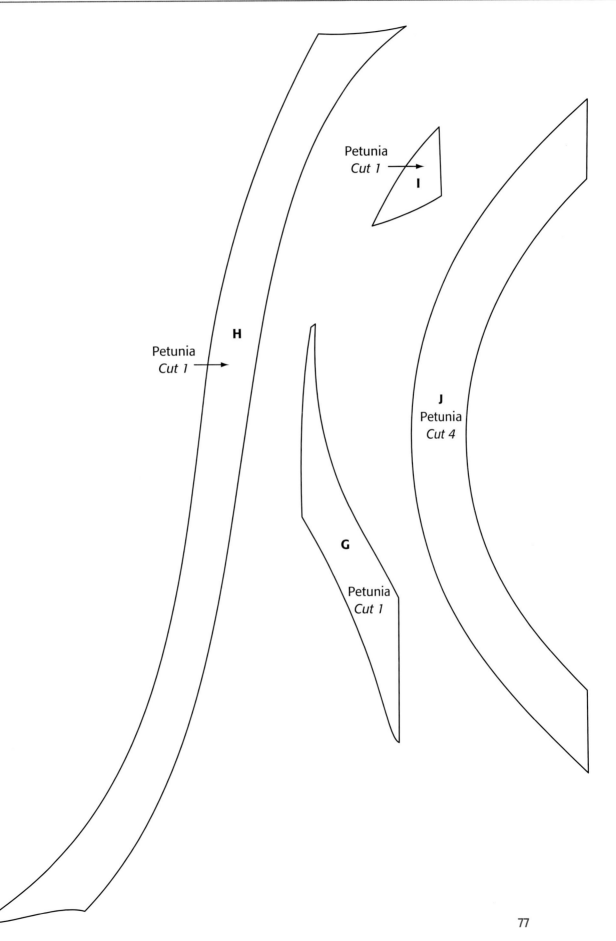

Petunia
*Cut 1* →

**I**

**H**

Petunia
*Cut 1* →

**J**
Petunia
*Cut 4*

**G**

Petunia
*Cut 1*

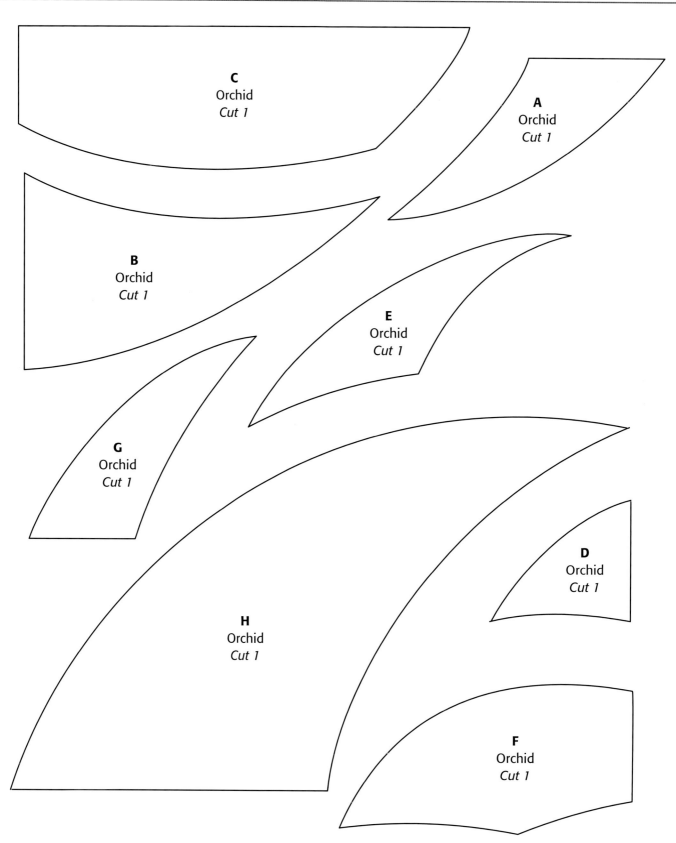

C
Orchid
*Cut 1*

A
Orchid
*Cut 1*

B
Orchid
*Cut 1*

E
Orchid
*Cut 1*

G
Orchid
*Cut 1*

H
Orchid
*Cut 1*

D
Orchid
*Cut 1*

F
Orchid
*Cut 1*

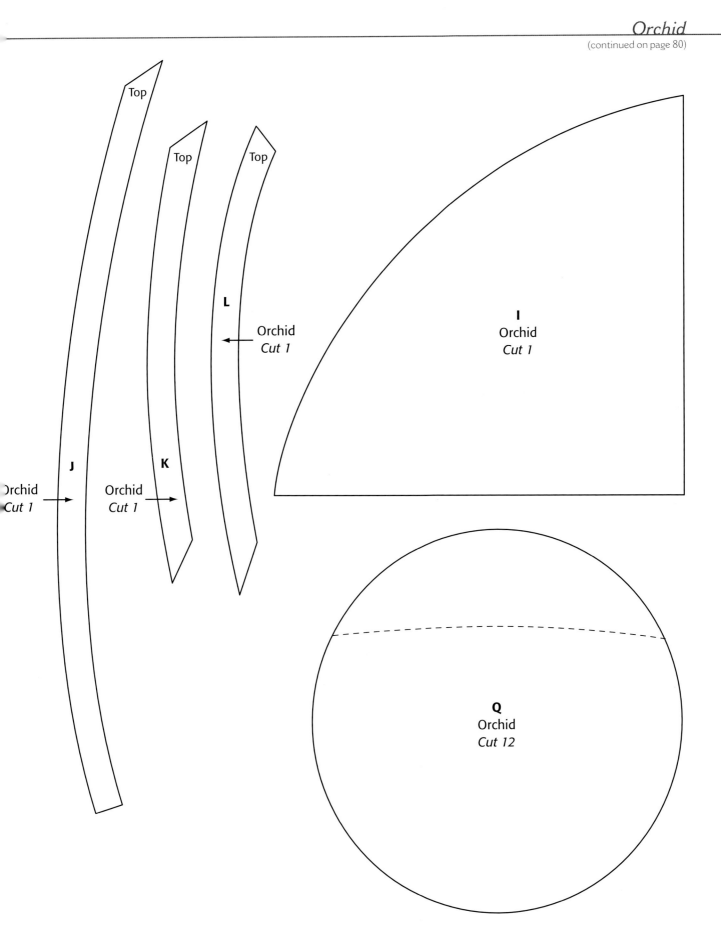

Top

Top

Top

L

Orchid
*Cut 1*

I
Orchid
*Cut 1*

J

K

Orchid
*Cut 1*

Orchid
*Cut 1*

Q
Orchid
*Cut 12*

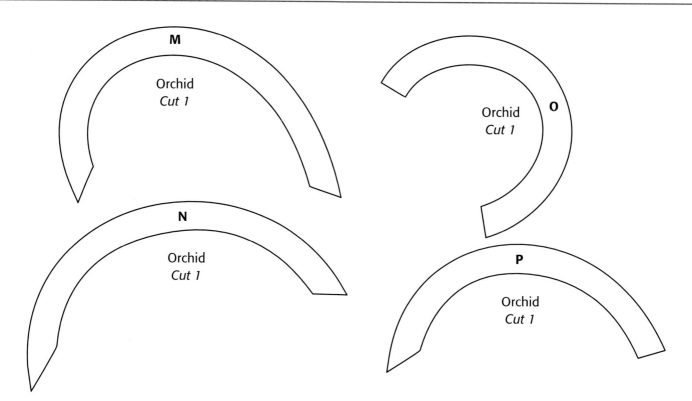

**M**

Orchid
*Cut 1*

**O**

Orchid
*Cut 1*

**N**

Orchid
*Cut 1*

**P**

Orchid
*Cut 1*

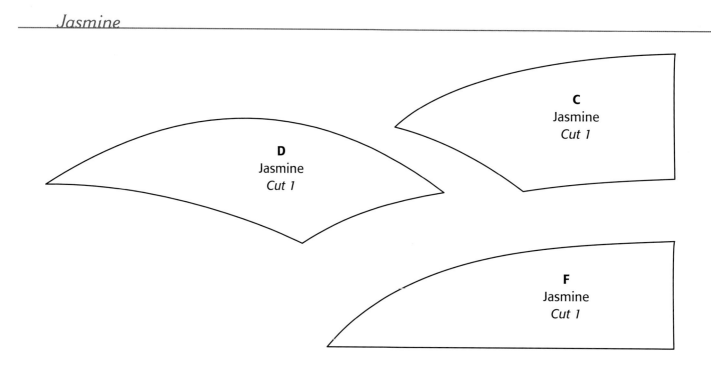

**D**
Jasmine
*Cut 1*

**C**
Jasmine
*Cut 1*

**F**
Jasmine
*Cut 1*

(continued on page 82)

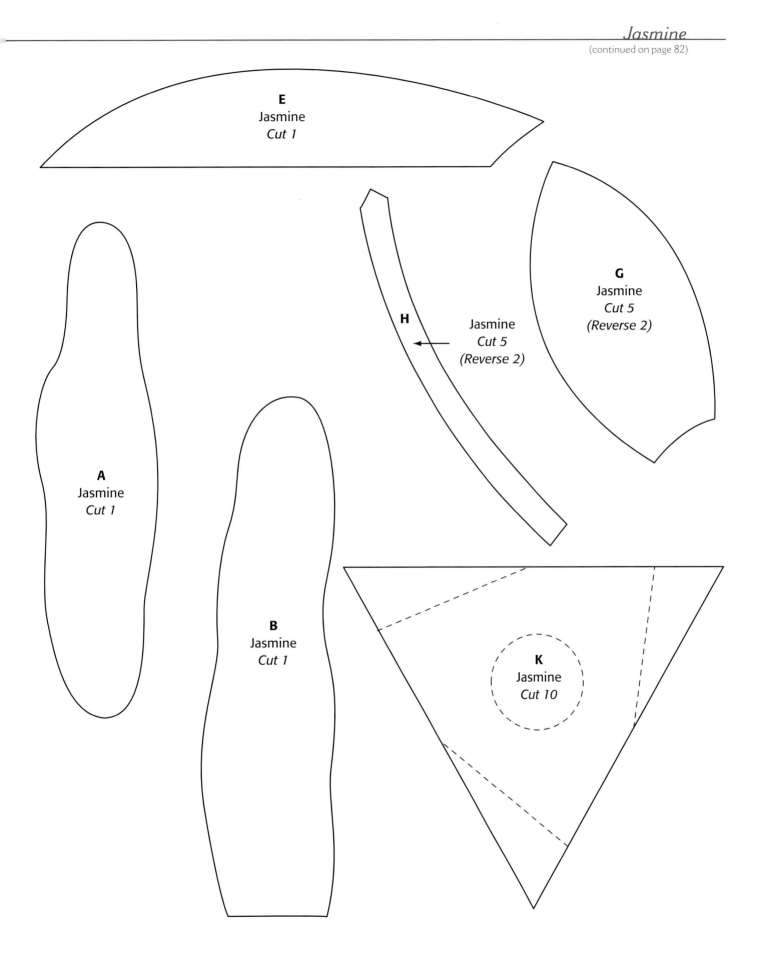

**E**
Jasmine
*Cut 1*

**G**
Jasmine
*Cut 5*
*(Reverse 2)*

**H**
Jasmine
*Cut 5*
*(Reverse 2)*

**A**
Jasmine
*Cut 1*

**B**
Jasmine
*Cut 1*

**K**
Jasmine
*Cut 10*

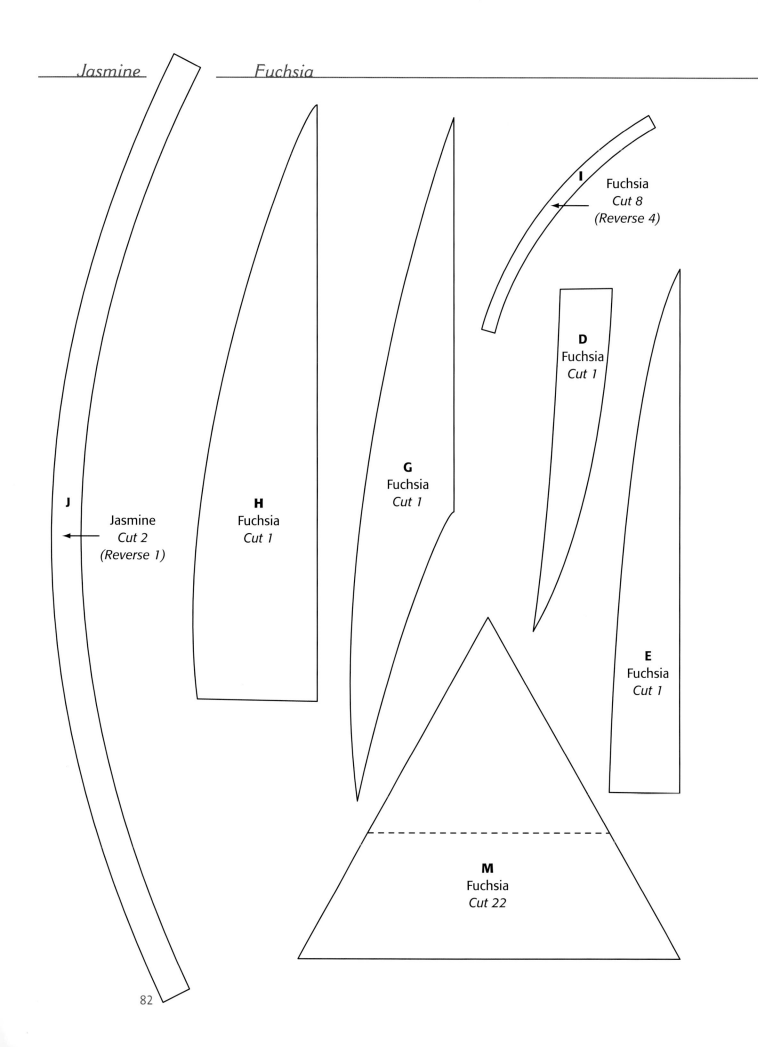

Jasmine    Fuchsia

I
Fuchsia
*Cut 8*
*(Reverse 4)*

D
Fuchsia
*Cut 1*

G
Fuchsia
*Cut 1*

J

Jasmine
*Cut 2*
*(Reverse 1)*

H
Fuchsia
*Cut 1*

E
Fuchsia
*Cut 1*

M
Fuchsia
*Cut 22*

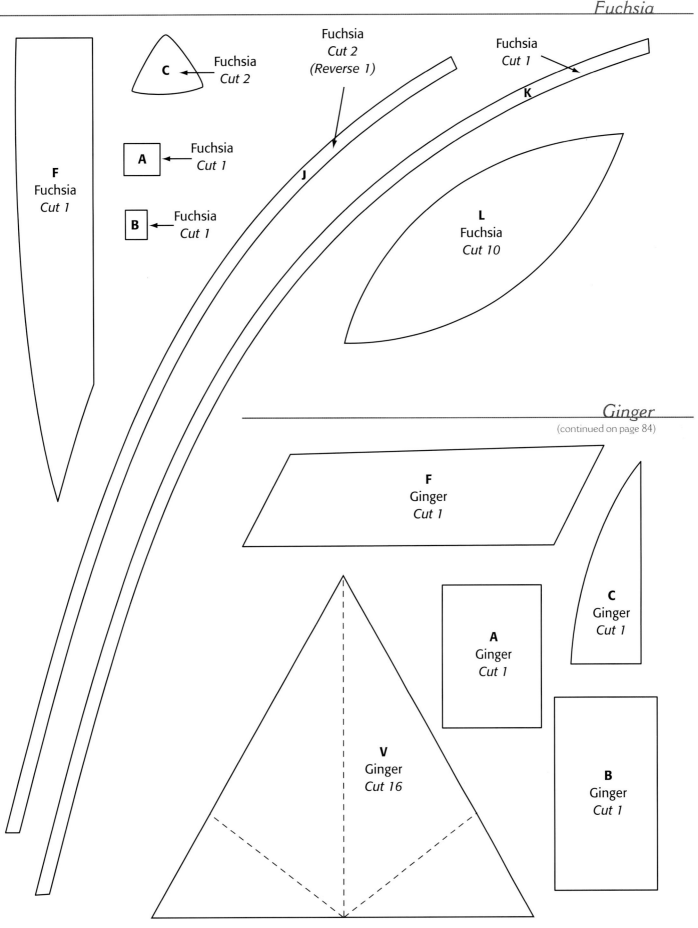

**F**
Fuchsia
*Cut 1*

**C** ← Fuchsia
*Cut 2*

Fuchsia
*Cut 2*
*(Reverse 1)*

Fuchsia
*Cut 1*

**A** ← Fuchsia
*Cut 1*

**B** ← Fuchsia
*Cut 1*

**J**

**K**

**L**
Fuchsia
*Cut 10*

(continued on page 84)

**F**
Ginger
*Cut 1*

**C**
Ginger
*Cut 1*

**A**
Ginger
*Cut 1*

**B**
Ginger
*Cut 1*

**V**
Ginger
*Cut 16*

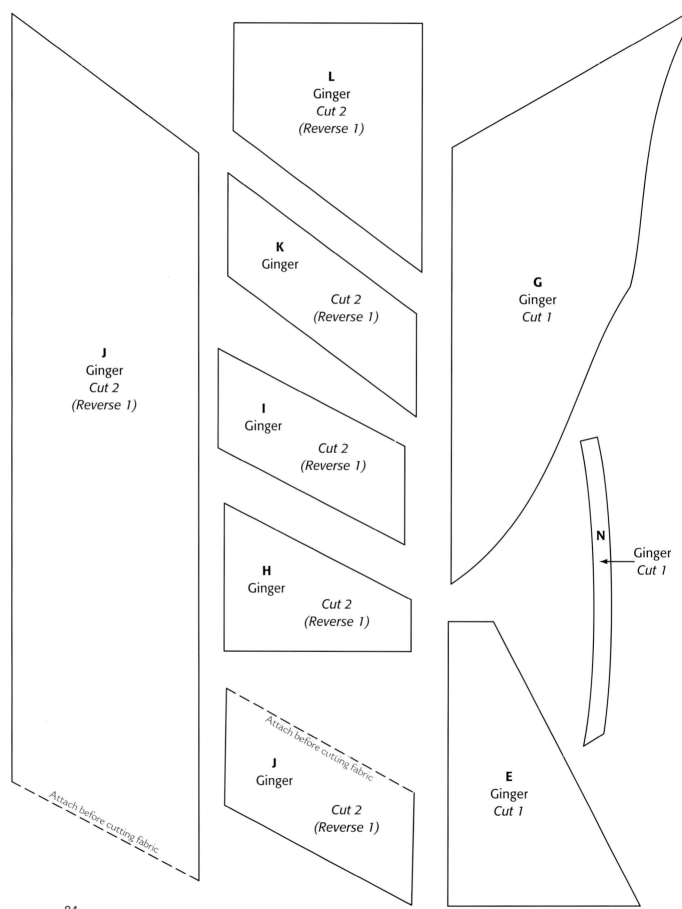

**L**
Ginger
*Cut 2*
*(Reverse 1)*

**K**
Ginger

*Cut 2*
*(Reverse 1)*

**J**
Ginger
*Cut 2*
*(Reverse 1)*

**I**
Ginger

*Cut 2*
*(Reverse 1)*

**H**
Ginger

*Cut 2*
*(Reverse 1)*

*Attach before cutting fabric*

**J**
Ginger

*Cut 2*
*(Reverse 1)*

**G**
Ginger
*Cut 1*

**N**
Ginger
*Cut 1*

**E**
Ginger
*Cut 1*

*Attach before cutting fabric*

84

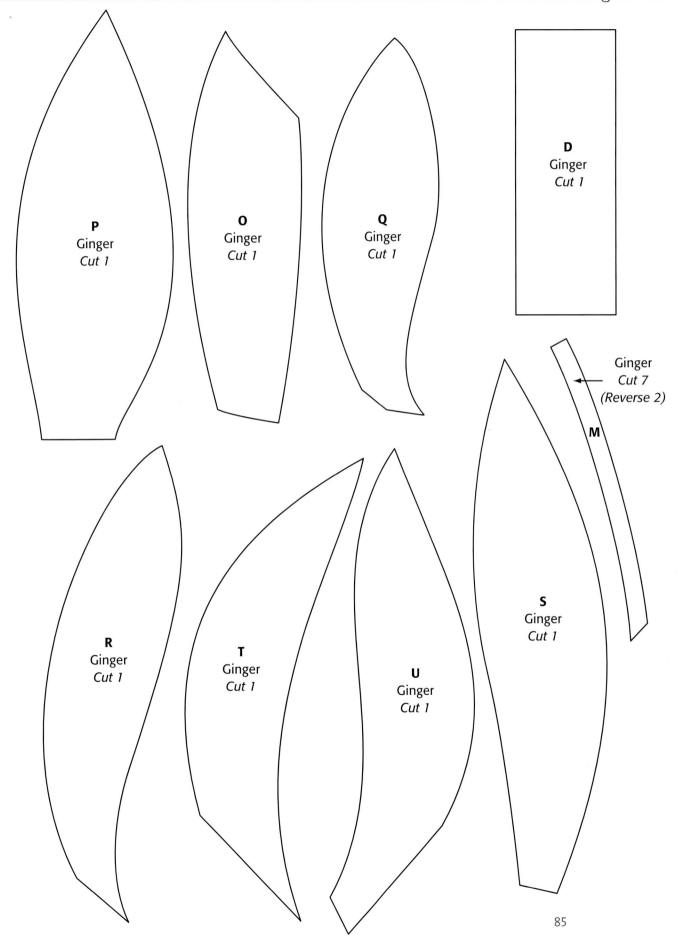

**P**
Ginger
*Cut 1*

**O**
Ginger
*Cut 1*

**Q**
Ginger
*Cut 1*

**D**
Ginger
*Cut 1*

Ginger
*Cut 7*
*(Reverse 2)*

**M**

**R**
Ginger
*Cut 1*

**T**
Ginger
*Cut 1*

**U**
Ginger
*Cut 1*

**S**
Ginger
*Cut 1*

85

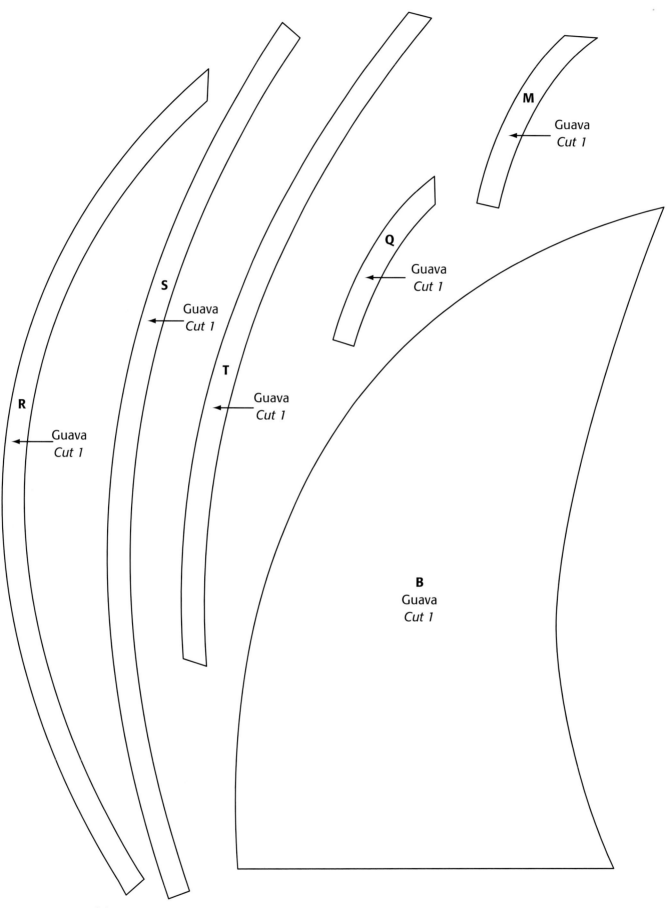

M
Guava
*Cut 1*

Q
Guava
*Cut 1*

S
Guava
*Cut 1*

T
Guava
*Cut 1*

R
Guava
*Cut 1*

B
Guava
*Cut 1*

(continued on page 88)

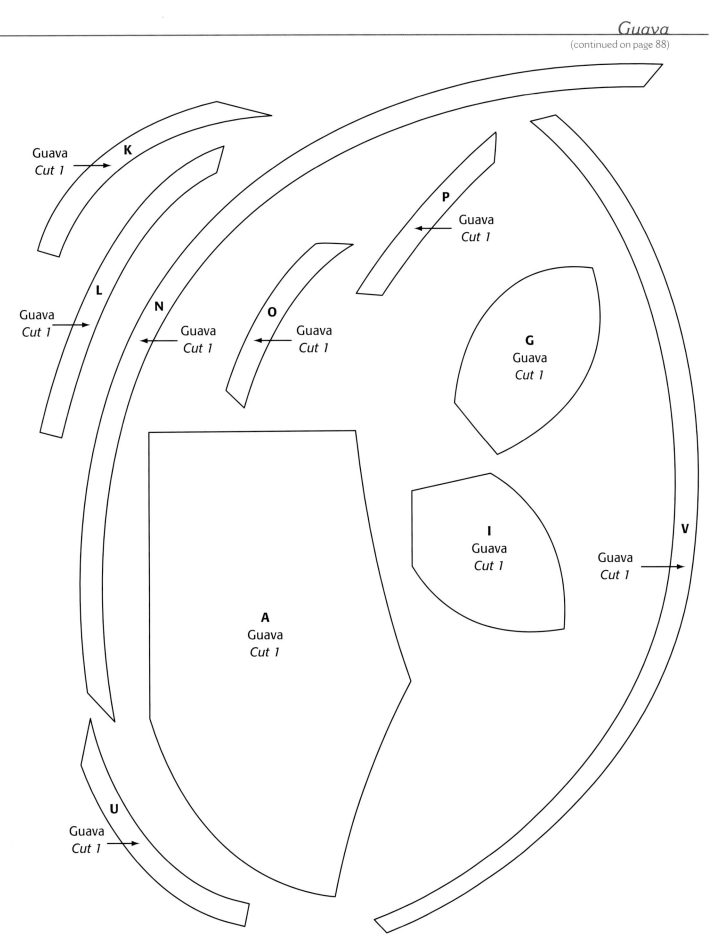

Guava
*Cut 1* **K**

**P**
Guava
*Cut 1*

Guava
*Cut 1* **L**

**N**
Guava
*Cut 1*

**O**
Guava
*Cut 1*

**G**
Guava
*Cut 1*

**A**
Guava
*Cut 1*

**I**
Guava
*Cut 1*

**V**
Guava
*Cut 1*

**U**
Guava
*Cut 1*

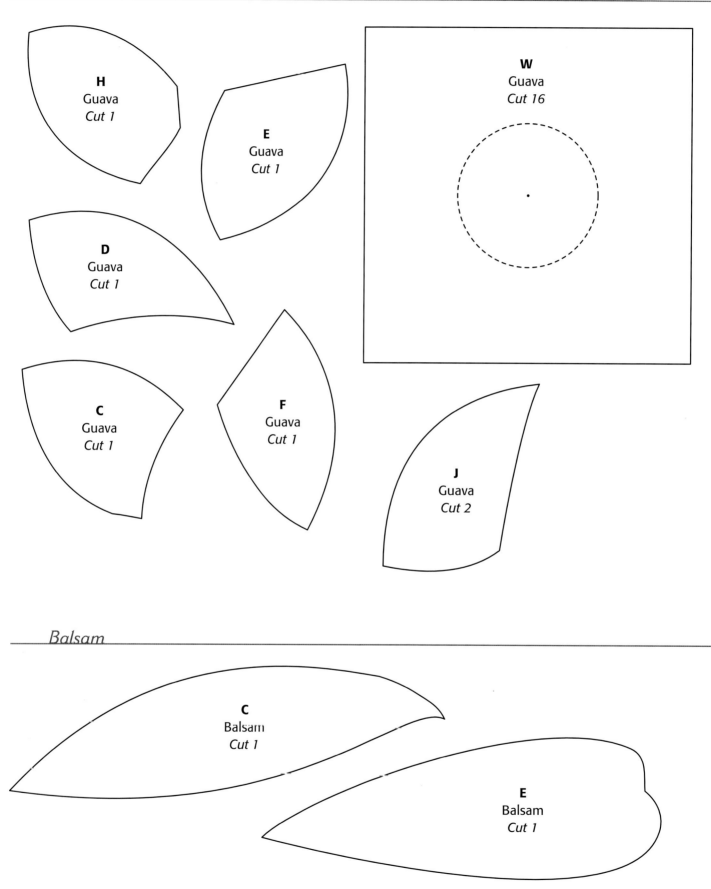

**H**
Guava
*Cut 1*

**E**
Guava
*Cut 1*

**W**
Guava
*Cut 16*

**D**
Guava
*Cut 1*

**C**
Guava
*Cut 1*

**F**
Guava
*Cut 1*

**J**
Guava
*Cut 2*

*Balsam*

**C**
Balsam
*Cut 1*

**E**
Balsam
*Cut 1*

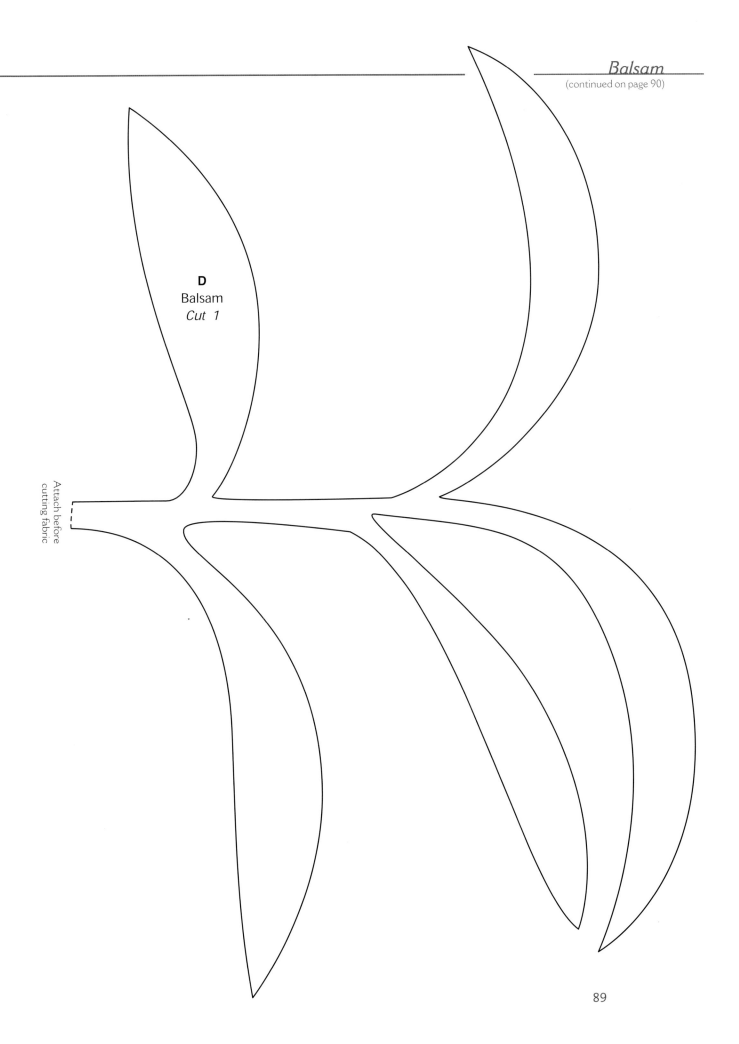

(continued on page 90)

**D**
Balsam
*Cut  1*

Attach before
cutting fabric

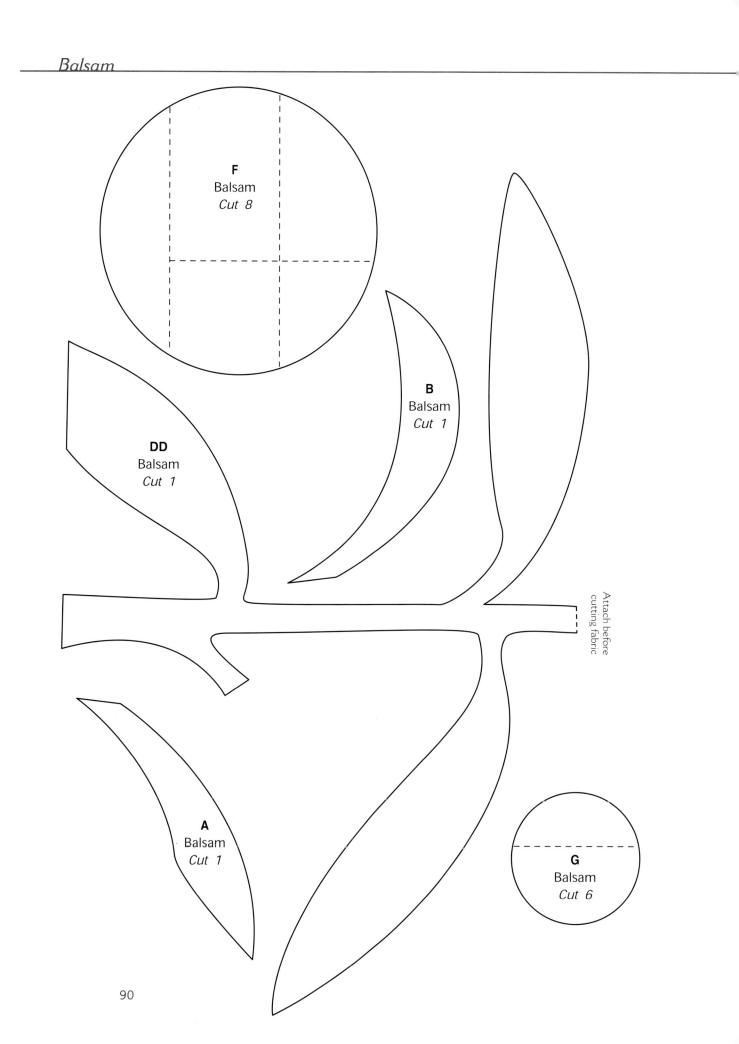

**F**
Balsam
*Cut 8*

**DD**
Balsam
*Cut 1*

**B**
Balsam
*Cut 1*

Attach before
cutting fabric

**A**
Balsam
*Cut 1*

**G**
Balsam
*Cut 6*

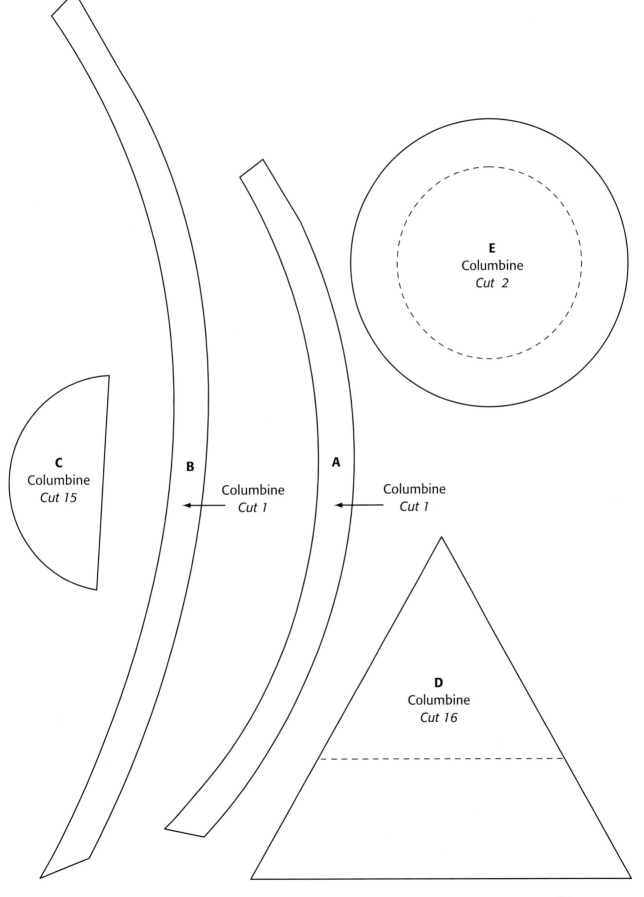

**E**
Columbine
*Cut 2*

**C**
Columbine
*Cut 15*

**B**

**A**

Columbine
*Cut 1*

Columbine
*Cut 1*

**D**
Columbine
*Cut 16*

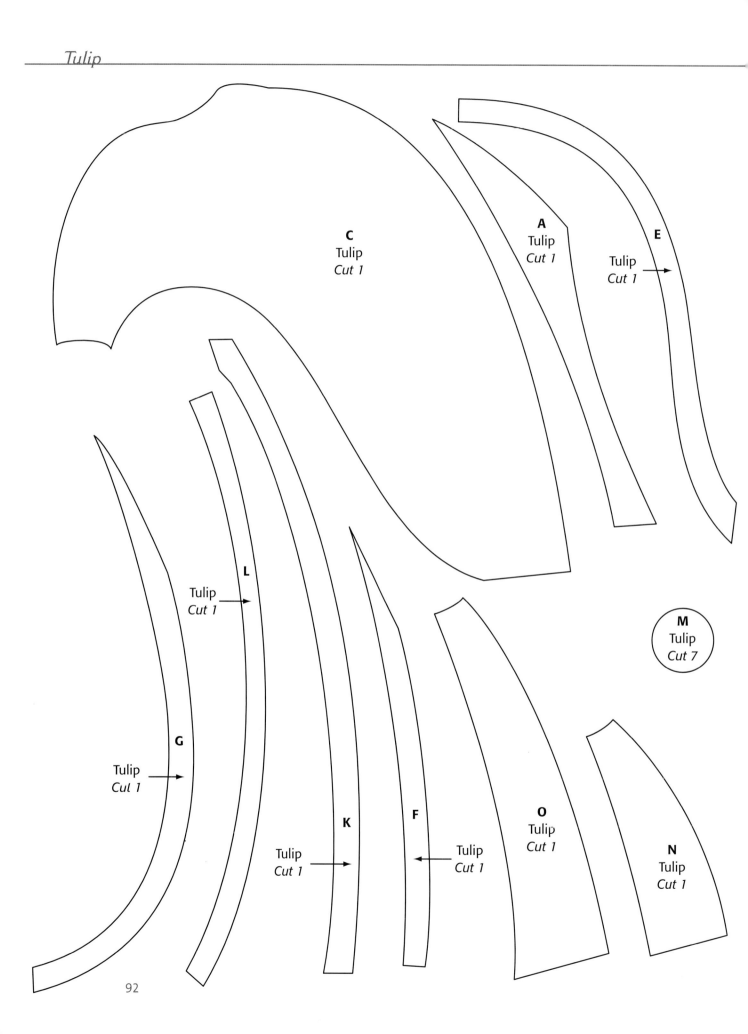

**C**
Tulip
*Cut 1*

**A**
Tulip
*Cut 1*

**E**
Tulip
*Cut 1* →

**M**
Tulip
*Cut 7*

**L**
Tulip
*Cut 1* →

**G**
Tulip
*Cut 1* →

**K**
Tulip
*Cut 1* →

**F**
← Tulip
*Cut 1*

**O**
Tulip
*Cut 1*

**N**
Tulip
*Cut 1*

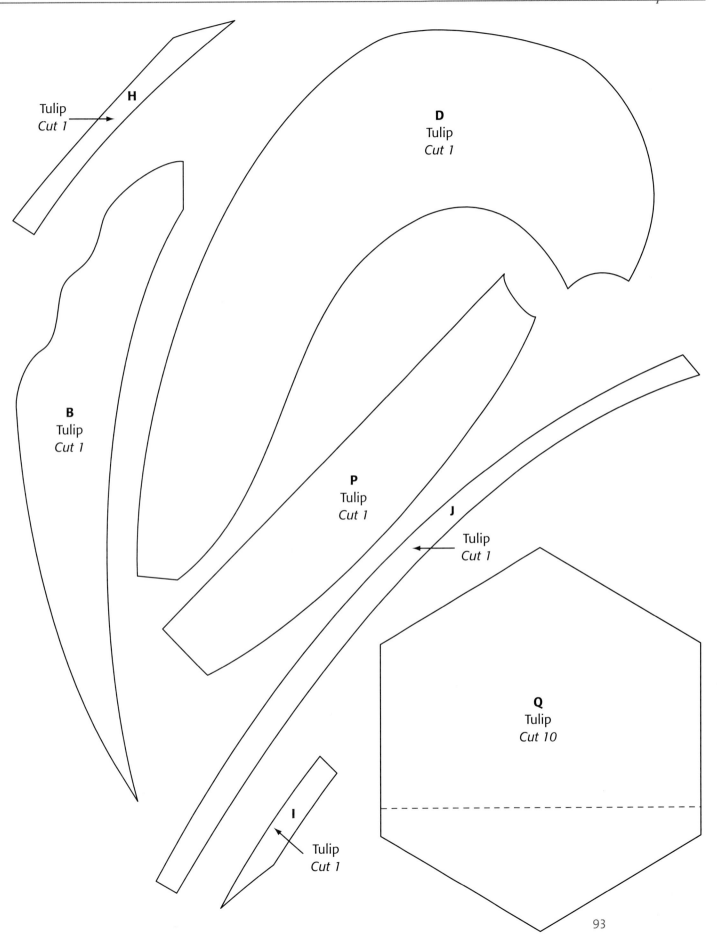

**H**
Tulip
*Cut 1*

**D**
Tulip
*Cut 1*

**B**
Tulip
*Cut 1*

**P**
Tulip
*Cut 1*

**J**
Tulip
*Cut 1*

**Q**
Tulip
*Cut 10*

**I**
Tulip
*Cut 1*

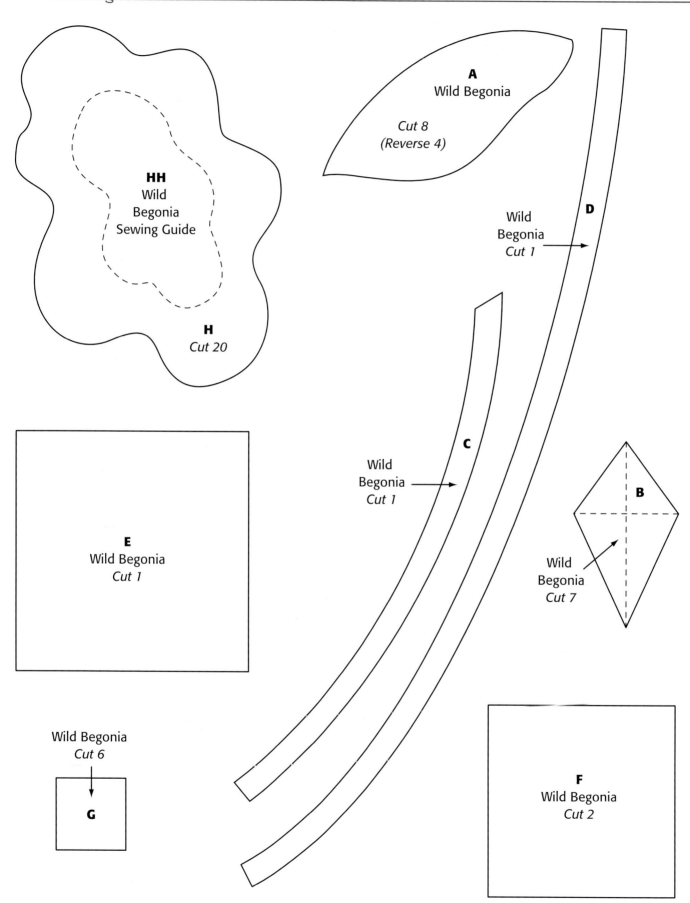

**HH**
Wild
Begonia
Sewing Guide

**H**
*Cut 20*

**A**
Wild Begonia

*Cut 8*
*(Reverse 4)*

Wild
Begonia
*Cut 1* → **D**

Wild
Begonia
*Cut 1* → **C**

**B**

Wild
Begonia
*Cut 7*

**E**
Wild Begonia
*Cut 1*

Wild Begonia
*Cut 6*

↓

**G**

**F**
Wild Begonia
*Cut 2*

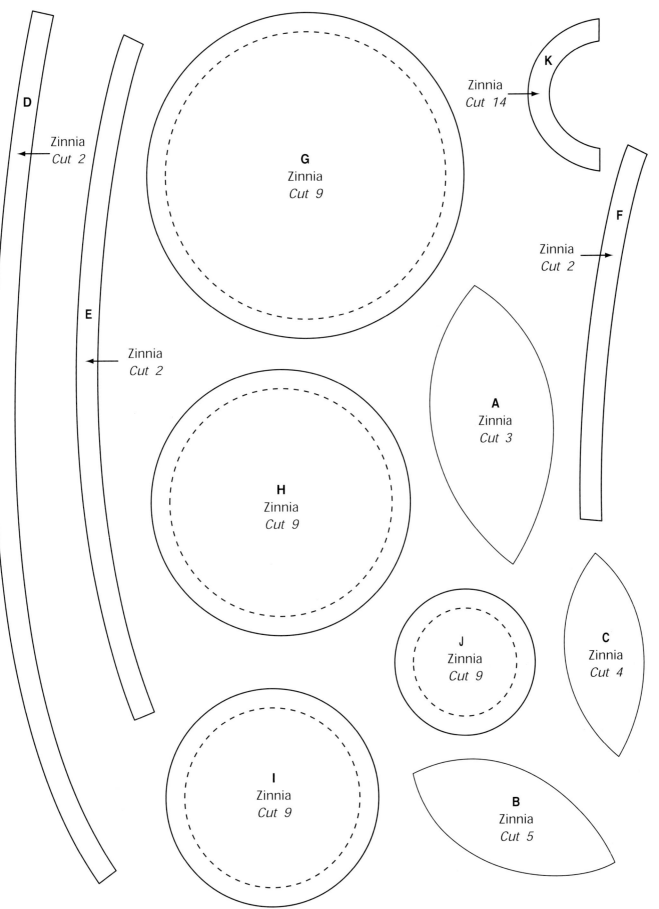

D

Zinnia
*Cut 2*

E

Zinnia
*Cut 2*

K

Zinnia
*Cut 14*

**G**
Zinnia
*Cut 9*

F

Zinnia
*Cut 2*

**A**
Zinnia
*Cut 3*

**H**
Zinnia
*Cut 9*

**C**
Zinnia
*Cut 4*

**J**
Zinnia
*Cut 9*

**I**
Zinnia
*Cut 9*

**B**
Zinnia
*Cut 5*

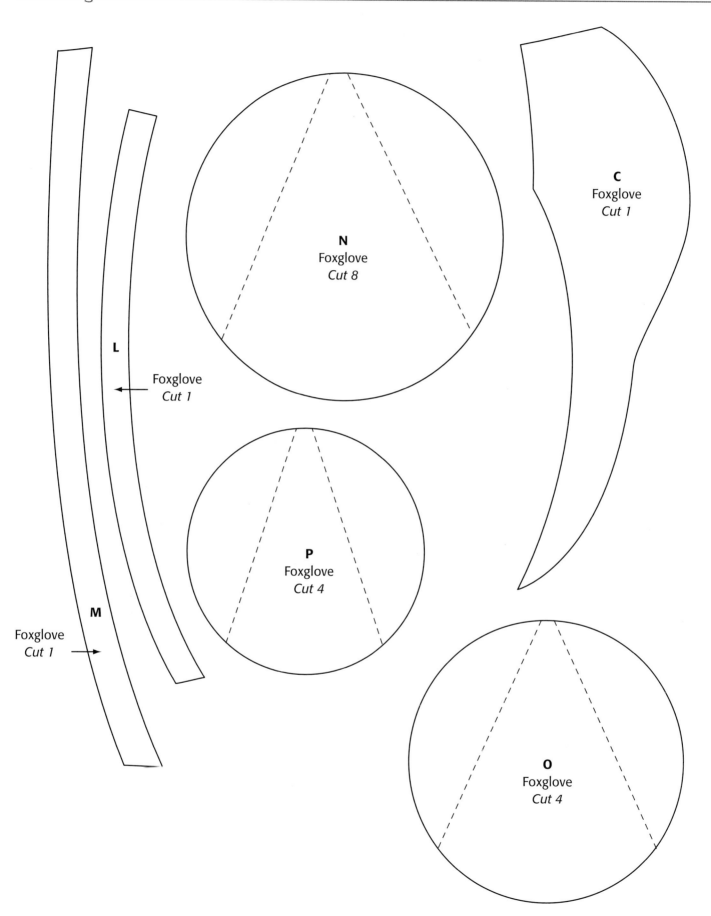

**N**
Foxglove
*Cut 8*

**C**
Foxglove
*Cut 1*

**L**

Foxglove
*Cut 1*

**P**
Foxglove
*Cut 4*

**M**

Foxglove
*Cut 1*

**O**
Foxglove
*Cut 4*

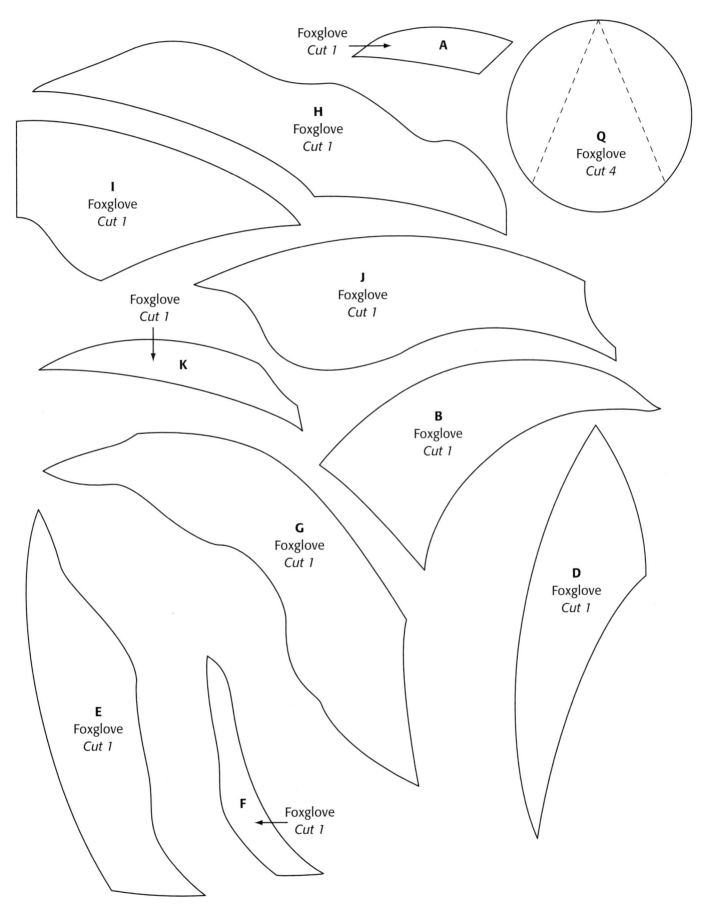

Foxglove
*Cut 1* →  **A**

**Q**
Foxglove
*Cut 4*

**H**
Foxglove
*Cut 1*

**I**
Foxglove
*Cut 1*

Foxglove
*Cut 1* ↓  **K**

**J**
Foxglove
*Cut 1*

**B**
Foxglove
*Cut 1*

**G**
Foxglove
*Cut 1*

**D**
Foxglove
*Cut 1*

**E**
Foxglove
*Cut 1*

**F** ← Foxglove
*Cut 1*

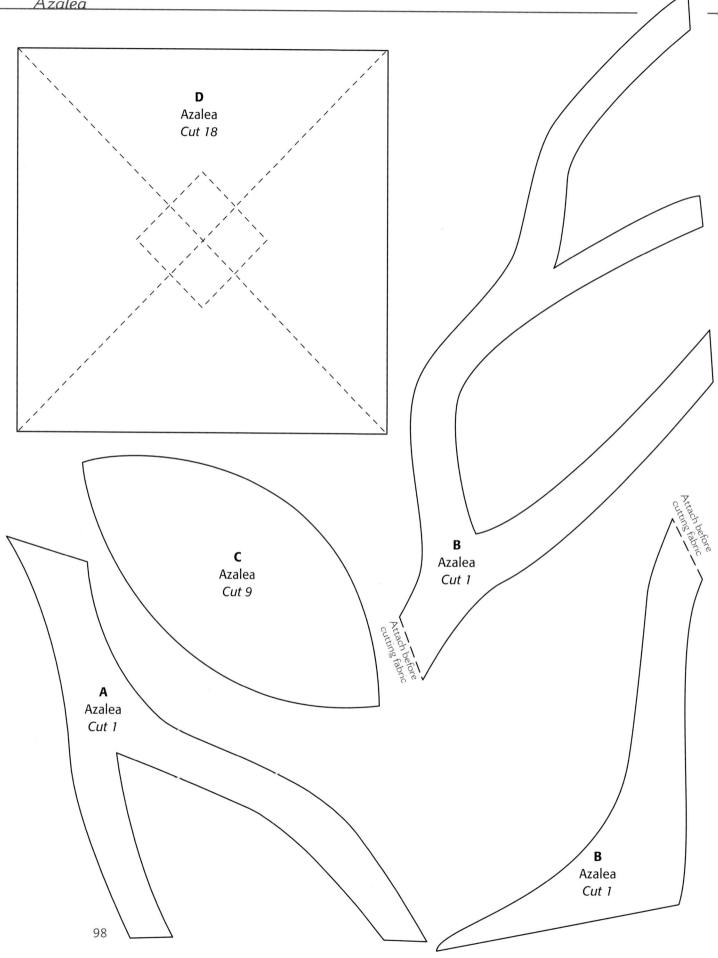

**D**
Azalea
*Cut 18*

**C**
Azalea
*Cut 9*

**B**
Azalea
*Cut 1*

Attach before cutting fabric

Attach before cutting fabric

**A**
Azalea
*Cut 1*

**B**
Azalea
*Cut 1*

98

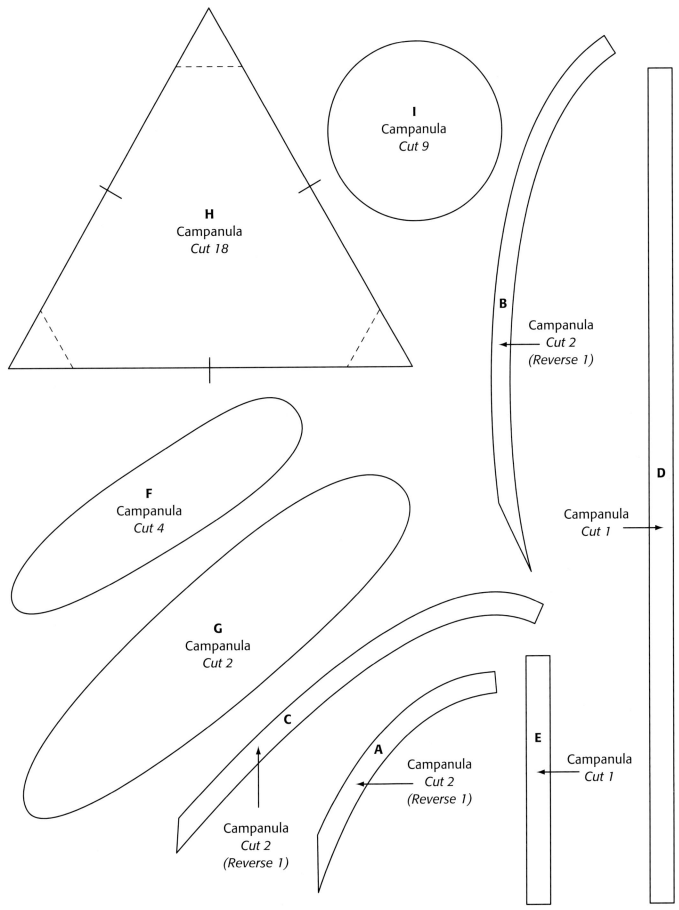

**I**
Campanula
*Cut 9*

**H**
Campanula
*Cut 18*

**B**
Campanula
*Cut 2*
*(Reverse 1)*

**D**
Campanula
*Cut 1*

**F**
Campanula
*Cut 4*

**G**
Campanula
*Cut 2*

**C**
Campanula
*Cut 2*
*(Reverse 1)*

**A**
Campanula
*Cut 2*
*(Reverse 1)*

**E**
Campanula
*Cut 1*

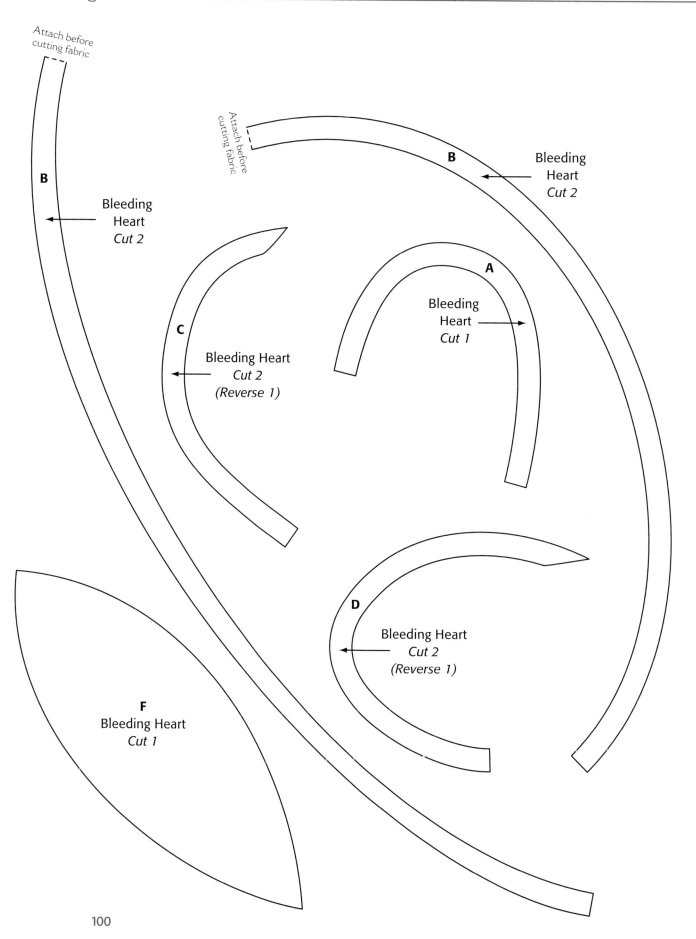

Attach before cutting fabric

**B**

Bleeding
Heart
*Cut 2*

Attach before cutting fabric

**B**

Bleeding
Heart
*Cut 2*

**A**

Bleeding
Heart
*Cut 1*

**C**

Bleeding Heart
*Cut 2*
*(Reverse 1)*

**D**

Bleeding Heart
*Cut 2*
*(Reverse 1)*

**F**
Bleeding Heart
*Cut 1*

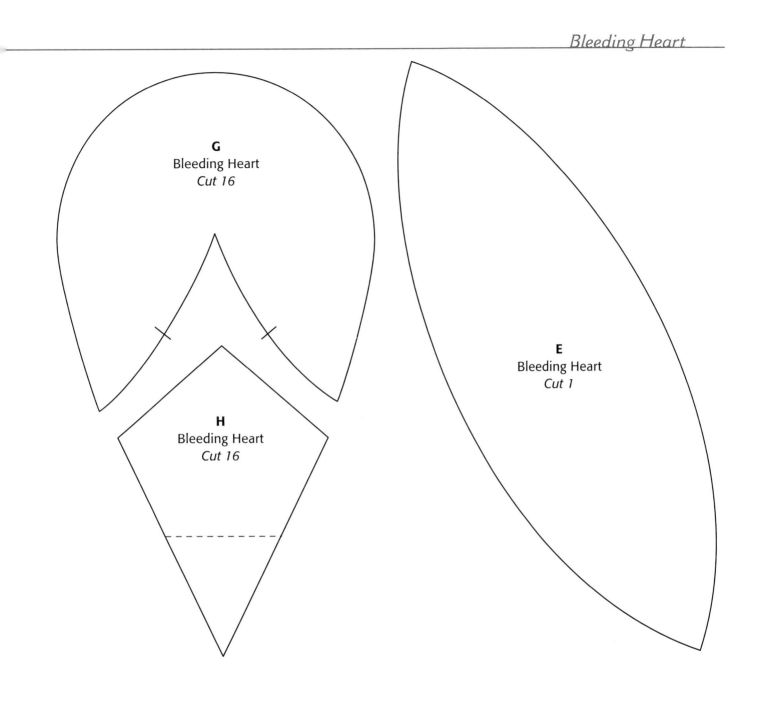

**G**
Bleeding Heart
*Cut 16*

**E**
Bleeding Heart
*Cut 1*

**H**
Bleeding Heart
*Cut 16*

(continued on page 102)

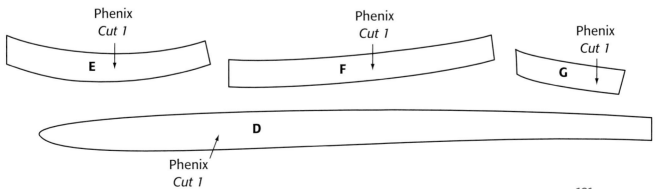

Phenix
*Cut 1*

Phenix
*Cut 1*

Phenix
*Cut 1*

**E**

**F**

**G**

**D**

Phenix
*Cut 1*

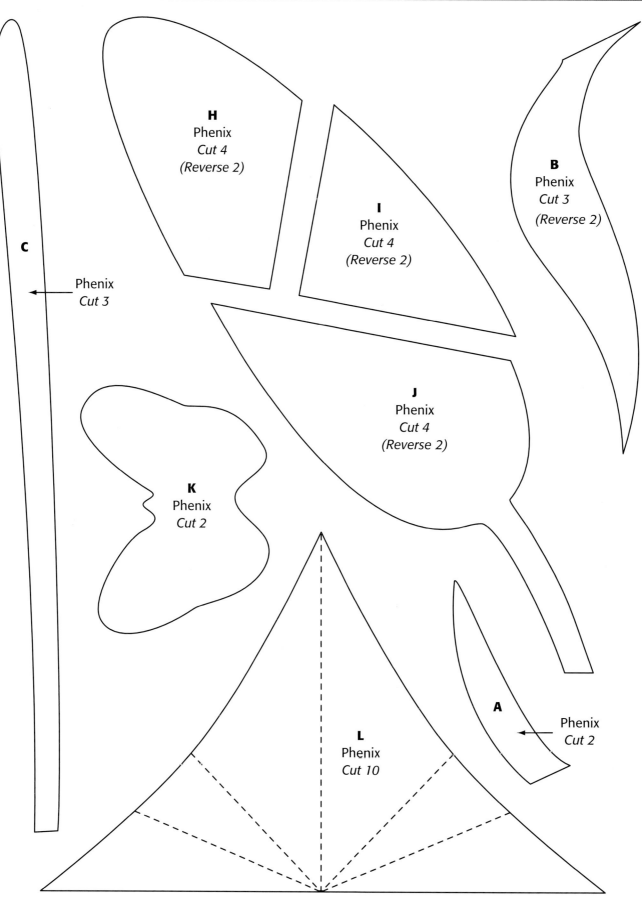

**H**
Phenix
*Cut 4*
*(Reverse 2)*

**I**
Phenix
*Cut 4*
*(Reverse 2)*

**B**
Phenix
*Cut 3*
*(Reverse 2)*

**C**

Phenix
*Cut 3*

**J**
Phenix
*Cut 4*
*(Reverse 2)*

**K**
Phenix
*Cut 2*

**A**

Phenix
*Cut 2*

**L**
Phenix
*Cut 10*

(continued on page 104)

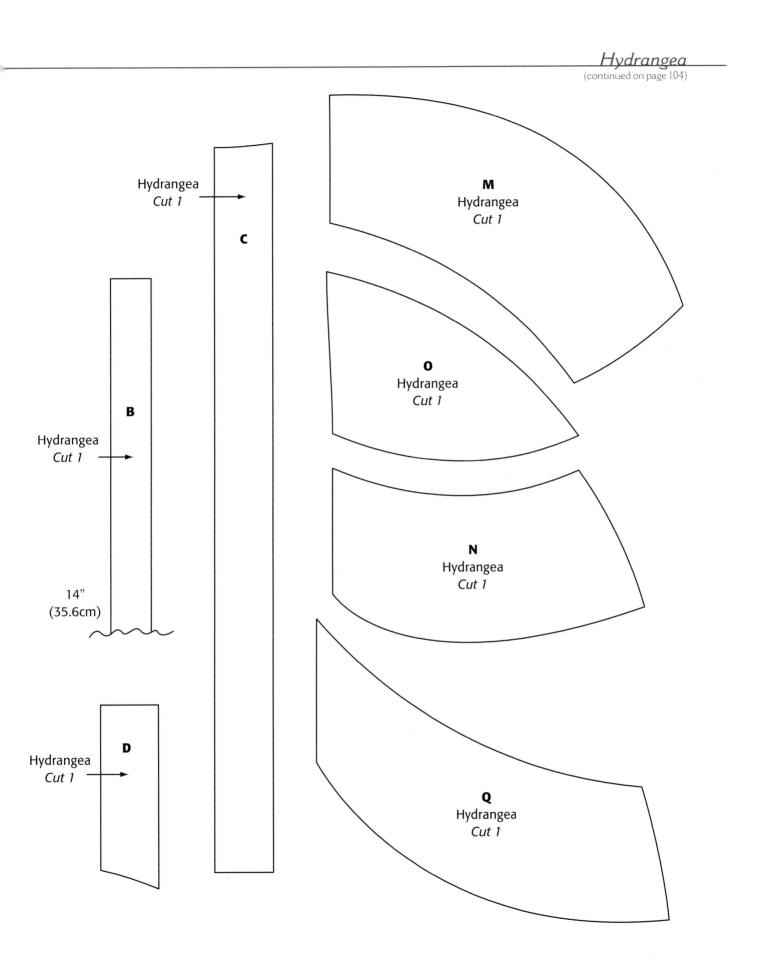

Hydrangea
*Cut 1* →

**C**

**M**
Hydrangea
*Cut 1*

**B**

Hydrangea
*Cut 1* →

**O**
Hydrangea
*Cut 1*

**N**
Hydrangea
*Cut 1*

14"
(35.6cm)

**D**

Hydrangea
*Cut 1* →

**Q**
Hydrangea
*Cut 1*

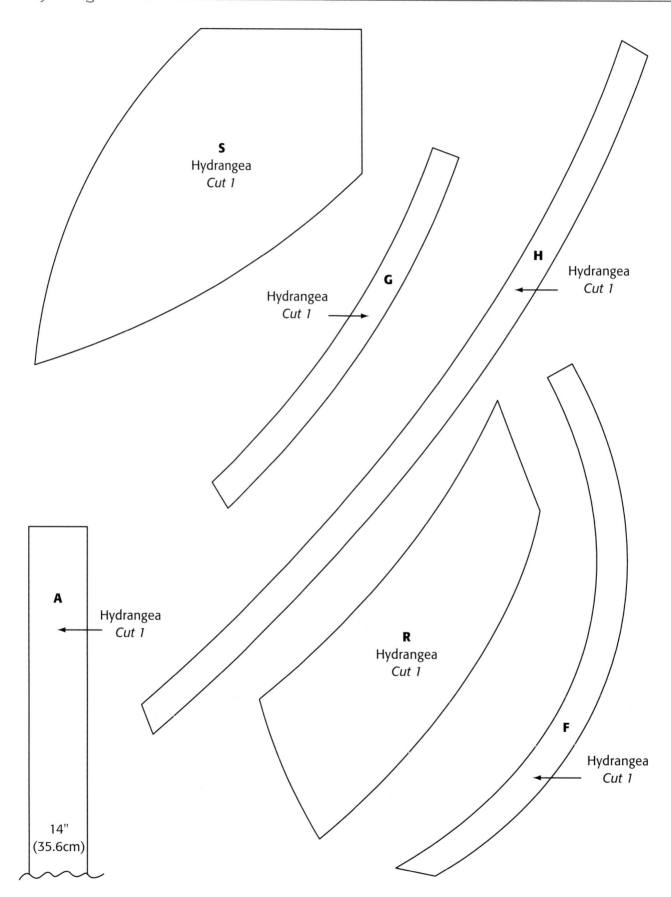

**S**
Hydrangea
*Cut 1*

**G**
Hydrangea
*Cut 1*

**H**
Hydrangea
*Cut 1*

**A**
Hydrangea
*Cut 1*

14"
(35.6cm)

**R**
Hydrangea
*Cut 1*

**F**
Hydrangea
*Cut 1*

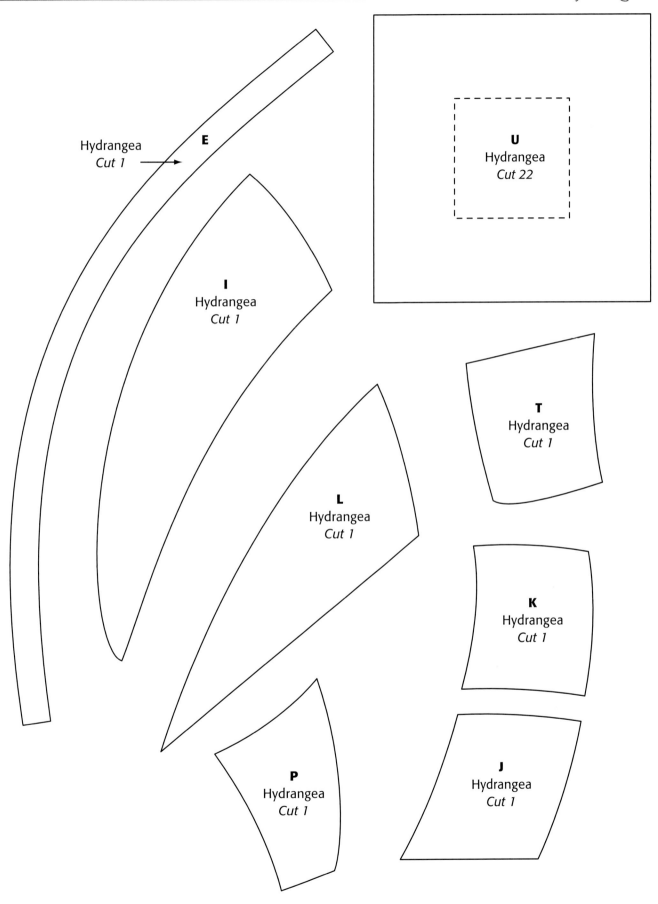

Hydrangea
*Cut 1* →

**E**

**I**
Hydrangea
*Cut 1*

**U**
Hydrangea
*Cut 22*

**T**
Hydrangea
*Cut 1*

**L**
Hydrangea
*Cut 1*

**K**
Hydrangea
*Cut 1*

**P**
Hydrangea
*Cut 1*

**J**
Hydrangea
*Cut 1*

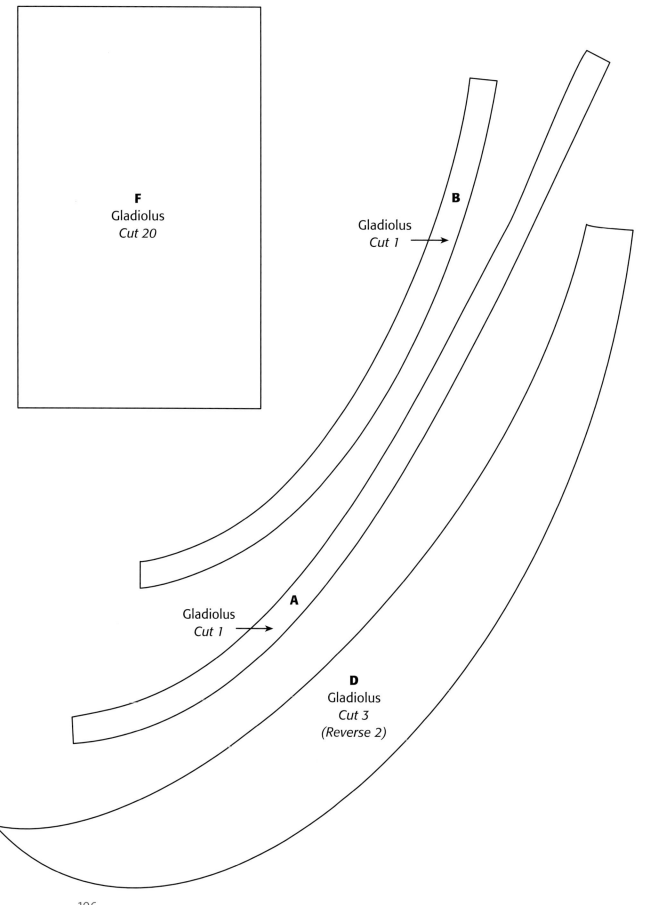

**F**
Gladiolus
*Cut 20*

**B**
Gladiolus
*Cut 1* →

**A**
Gladiolus
*Cut 1* →

**D**
Gladiolus
*Cut 3*
*(Reverse 2)*

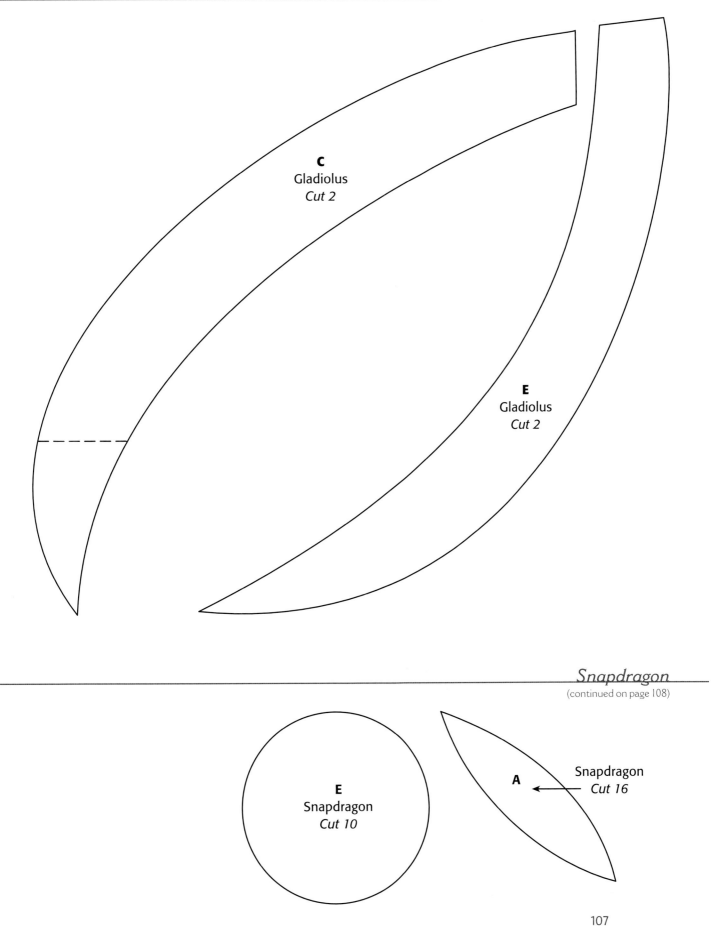

**C**
Gladiolus
*Cut 2*

**E**
Gladiolus
*Cut 2*

(continued on page 108)

**E**
Snapdragon
*Cut 10*

**A**

Snapdragon
*Cut 16*

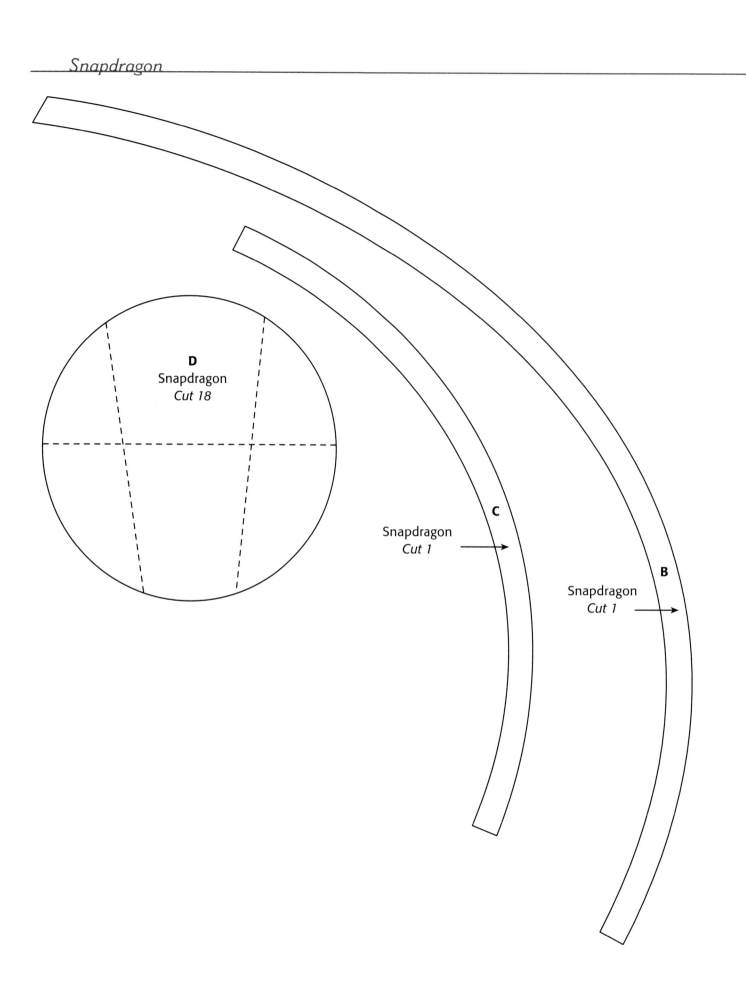

**D**
Snapdragon
*Cut 18*

Snapdragon
*Cut 1*

**C**

Snapdragon
*Cut 1*

**B**

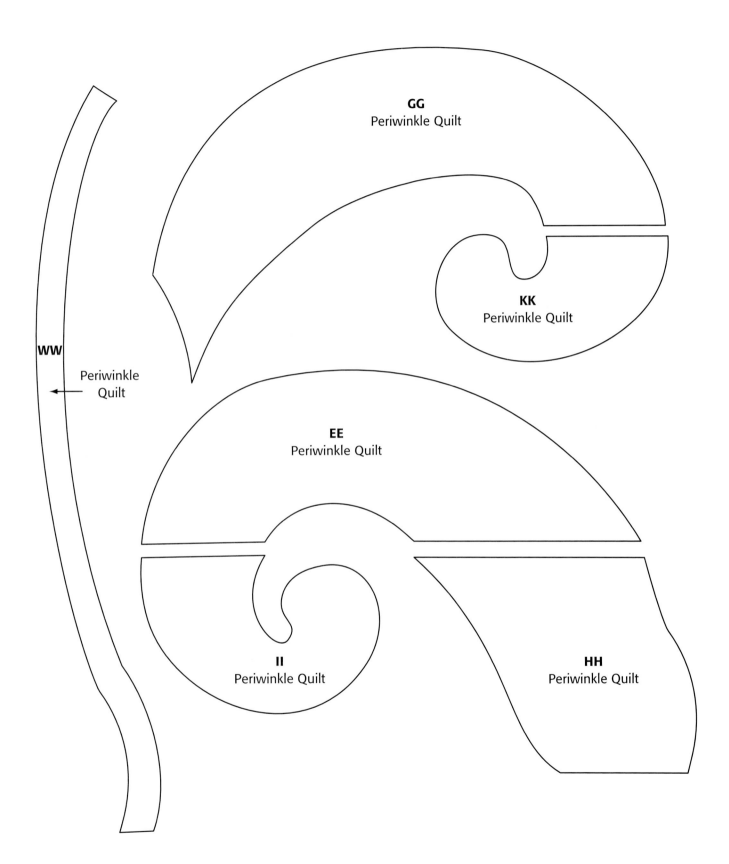

GG
Periwinkle Quilt

KK
Periwinkle Quilt

WW

Periwinkle
Quilt

EE
Periwinkle Quilt

II
Periwinkle Quilt

HH
Periwinkle Quilt

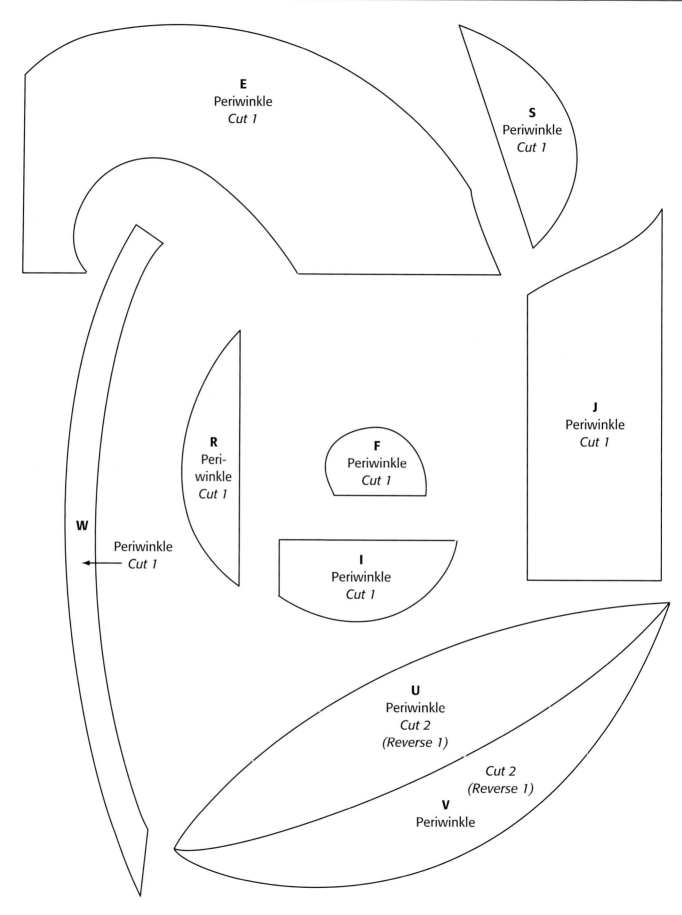

E
Periwinkle
*Cut 1*

S
Periwinkle
*Cut 1*

R
Peri-
winkle
*Cut 1*

F
Periwinkle
*Cut 1*

J
Periwinkle
*Cut 1*

W
Periwinkle
*Cut 1*

I
Periwinkle
*Cut 1*

U
Periwinkle
*Cut 2*
*(Reverse 1)*

*Cut 2*
*(Reverse 1)*

V
Periwinkle

(continued on page 112)

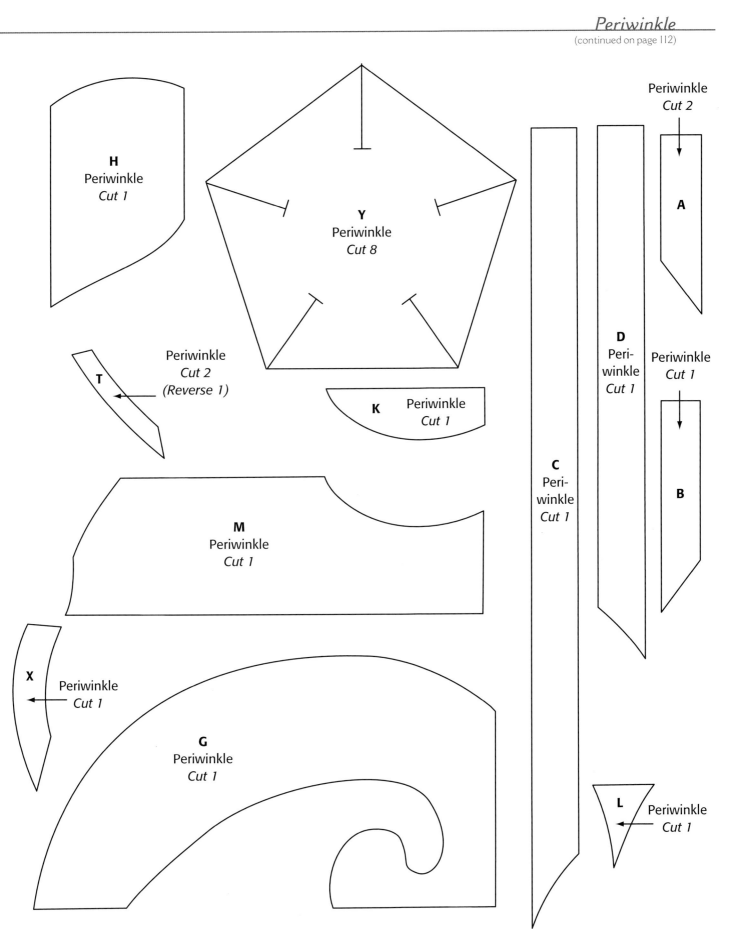

**H**
Periwinkle
*Cut 1*

**Y**
Periwinkle
*Cut 8*

Periwinkle
*Cut 2*

**A**

**T**

Periwinkle
*Cut 2*
*(Reverse 1)*

**K** Periwinkle
*Cut 1*

**D**
Peri-
winkle
*Cut 1*

Periwinkle
*Cut 1*

**B**

**C**
Peri-
winkle
*Cut 1*

**M**
Periwinkle
*Cut 1*

**X**

Periwinkle
*Cut 1*

**G**
Periwinkle
*Cut 1*

**L**

Periwinkle
*Cut 1*

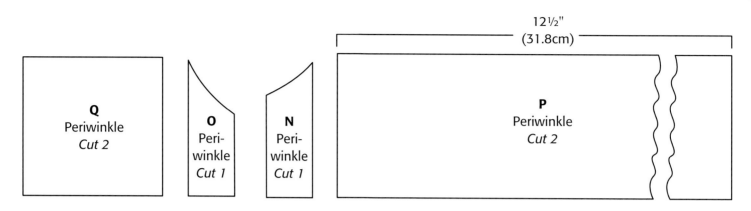

**Q**
Periwinkle
*Cut 2*

**O**
Peri-
winkle
*Cut 1*

**N**
Peri-
winkle
*Cut 1*

12½"
(31.8cm)

**P**
Periwinkle
*Cut 2*

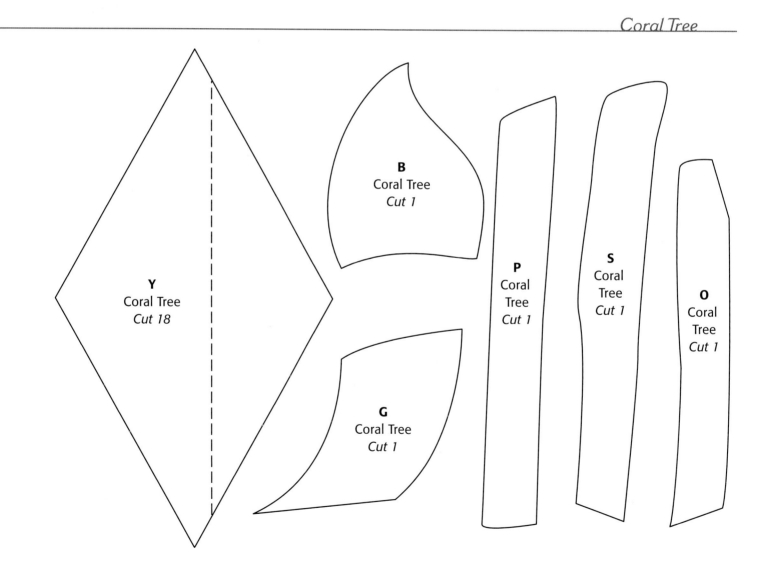

**Y**
Coral Tree
*Cut 18*

**B**
Coral Tree
*Cut 1*

**G**
Coral Tree
*Cut 1*

**P**
Coral
Tree
*Cut 1*

**S**
Coral
Tree
*Cut 1*

**O**
Coral
Tree
*Cut 1*

(continued on page 114)

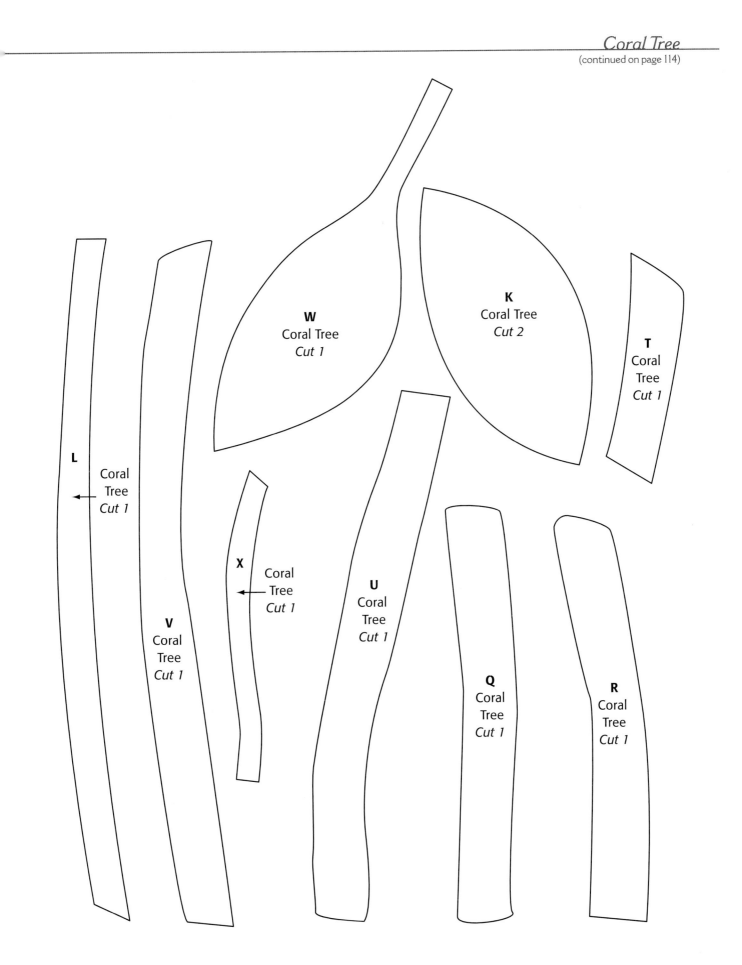

**W**
Coral Tree
*Cut 1*

**K**
Coral Tree
*Cut 2*

**T**
Coral
Tree
*Cut 1*

**L**
Coral
Tree
*Cut 1*

**X**
Coral
Tree
*Cut 1*

**U**
Coral
Tree
*Cut 1*

**V**
Coral
Tree
*Cut 1*

**Q**
Coral
Tree
*Cut 1*

**R**
Coral
Tree
*Cut 1*

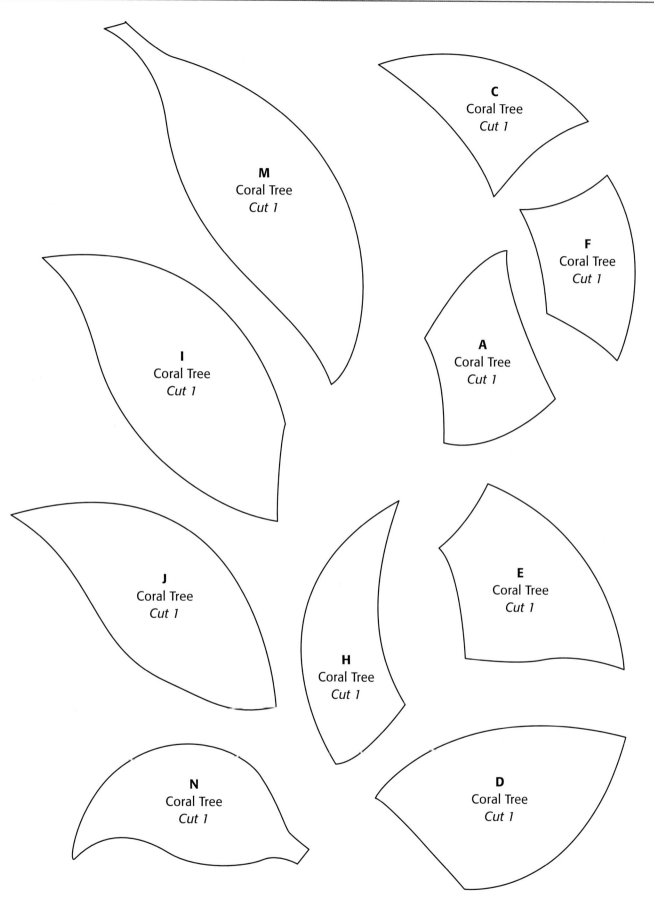

**M**
Coral Tree
*Cut 1*

**C**
Coral Tree
*Cut 1*

**F**
Coral Tree
*Cut 1*

**I**
Coral Tree
*Cut 1*

**A**
Coral Tree
*Cut 1*

**J**
Coral Tree
*Cut 1*

**E**
Coral Tree
*Cut 1*

**H**
Coral Tree
*Cut 1*

**N**
Coral Tree
*Cut 1*

**D**
Coral Tree
*Cut 1*

(continued on page 116)

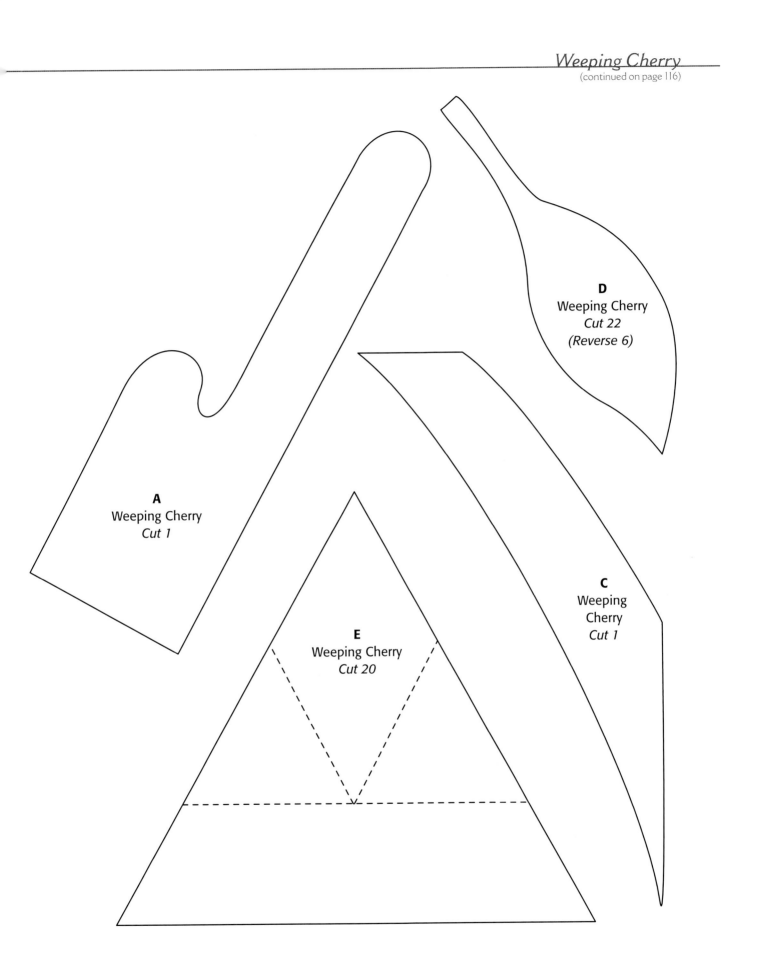

**D**
Weeping Cherry
*Cut 22*
*(Reverse 6)*

**A**
Weeping Cherry
*Cut 1*

**C**
Weeping
Cherry
*Cut 1*

**E**
Weeping Cherry
*Cut 20*

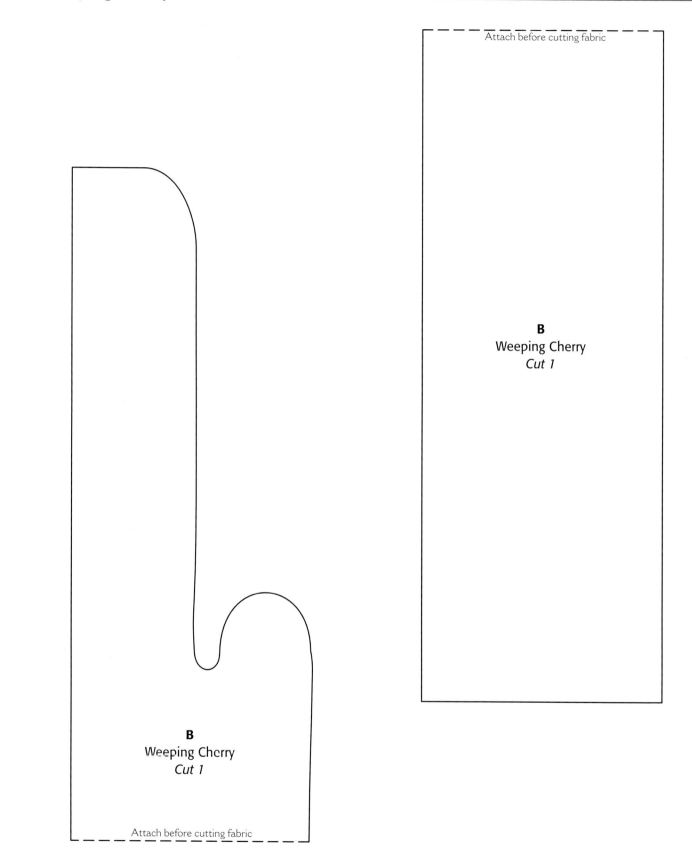

Attach before cutting fabric

**B**
Weeping Cherry
*Cut 1*

**B**
Weeping Cherry
*Cut 1*

Attach before cutting fabric

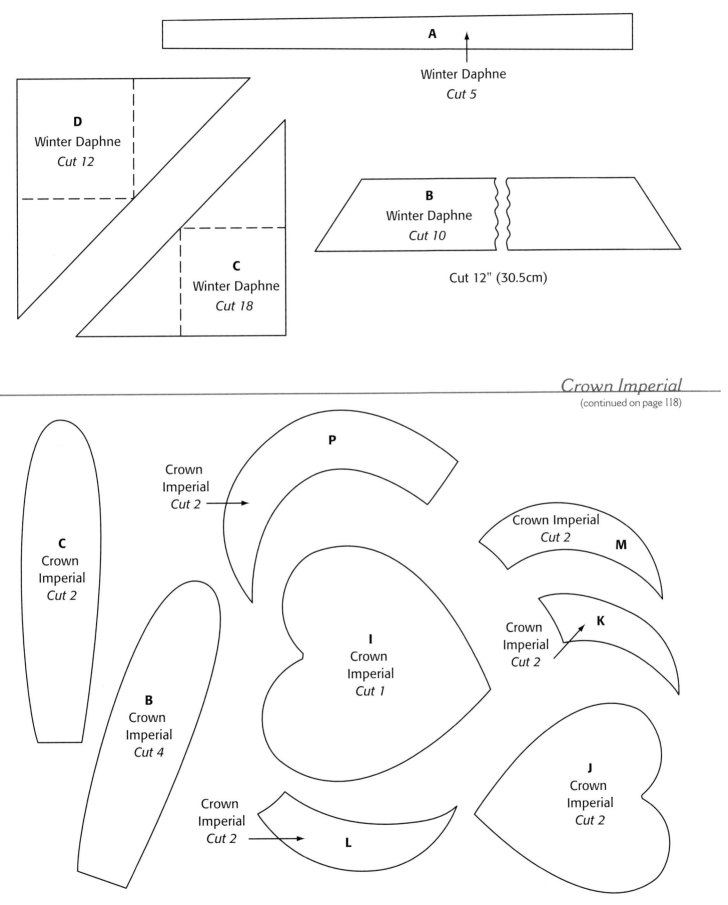

**A**

Winter Daphne
*Cut 5*

**D**
Winter Daphne
*Cut 12*

**C**
Winter Daphne
*Cut 18*

**B**
Winter Daphne
*Cut 10*

Cut 12" (30.5cm)

(continued on page 118)

**P**
Crown
Imperial
*Cut 2*

Crown Imperial
*Cut 2*
**M**

**C**
Crown
Imperial
*Cut 2*

**I**
Crown
Imperial
*Cut 1*

Crown
Imperial
*Cut 2*
**K**

**B**
Crown
Imperial
*Cut 4*

**J**
Crown
Imperial
*Cut 2*

Crown
Imperial
*Cut 2*
**L**

117

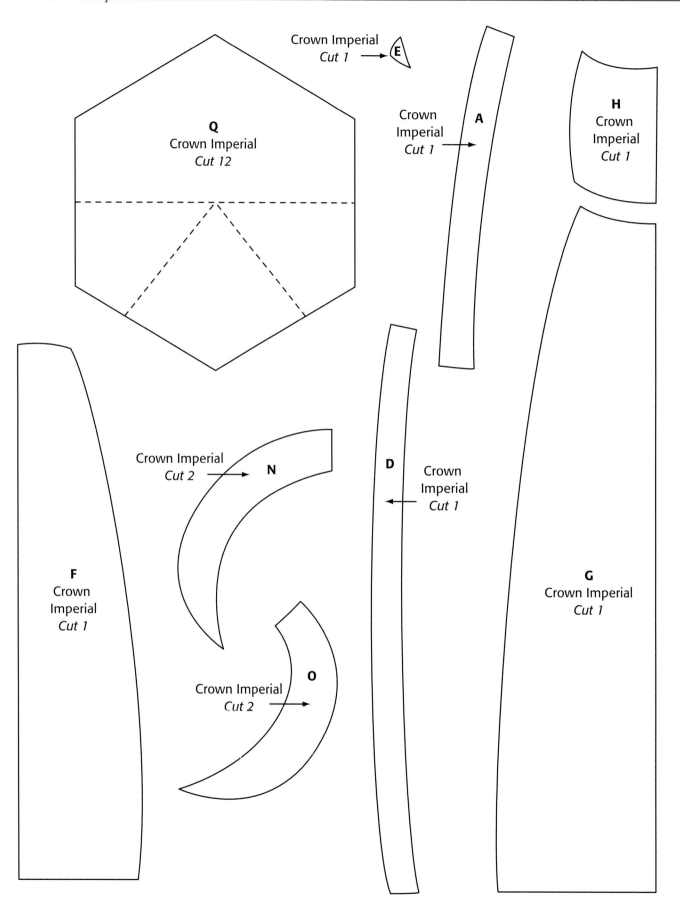

**Q**
Crown Imperial
*Cut 12*

Crown Imperial
*Cut 1* →  **E**

Crown
Imperial
*Cut 1* →  **A**

**H**
Crown
Imperial
*Cut 1*

Crown Imperial
*Cut 2* →  **N**

**D**
Crown
Imperial
*Cut 1* ←

**F**
Crown
Imperial
*Cut 1*

Crown Imperial
*Cut 2* →  **O**

**G**
Crown Imperial
*Cut 1*

(continued on page 120)

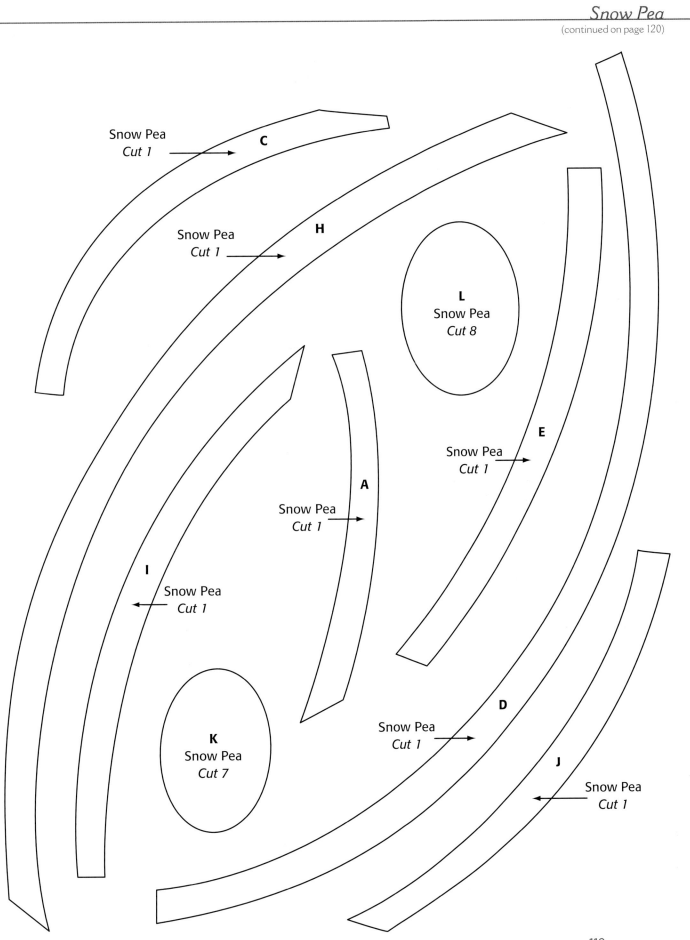

Snow Pea
*Cut 1*

**C**

Snow Pea
*Cut 1*

**H**

**L**
Snow Pea
*Cut 8*

**E**

Snow Pea
*Cut 1*

**A**

Snow Pea
*Cut 1*

**I**

Snow Pea
*Cut 1*

**D**

Snow Pea
*Cut 1*

**J**

Snow Pea
*Cut 1*

**K**
Snow Pea
*Cut 7*

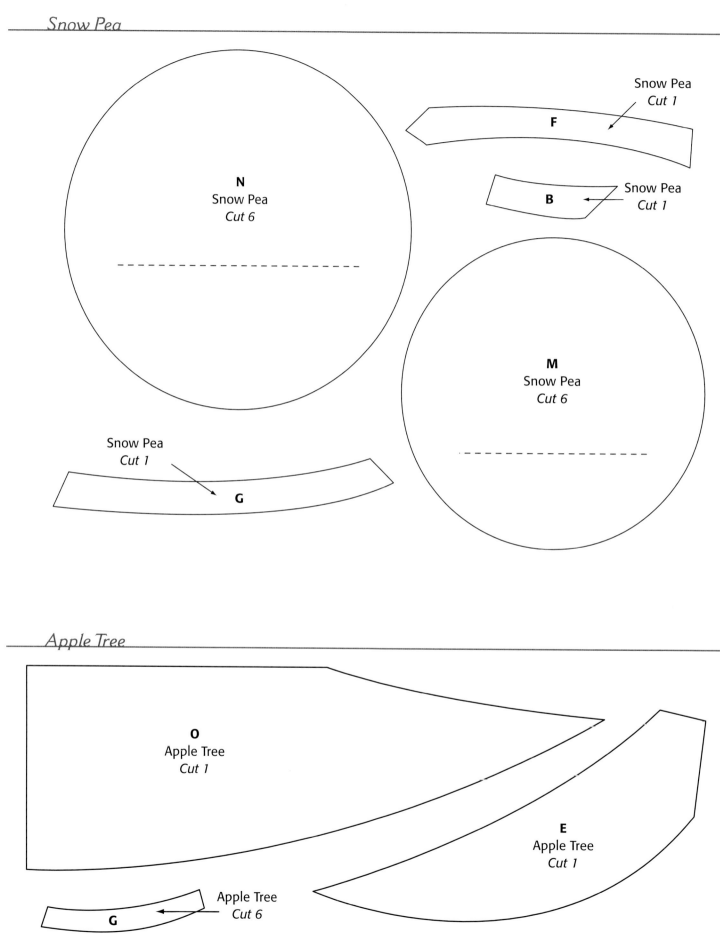

Snow Pea
*Cut 1*

**F**

Snow Pea
*Cut 1*

**B**

**N**
Snow Pea
*Cut 6*

**M**
Snow Pea
*Cut 6*

Snow Pea
*Cut 1*

**G**

*Apple Tree*

**O**
Apple Tree
*Cut 1*

**E**
Apple Tree
*Cut 1*

**G**

Apple Tree
*Cut 6*

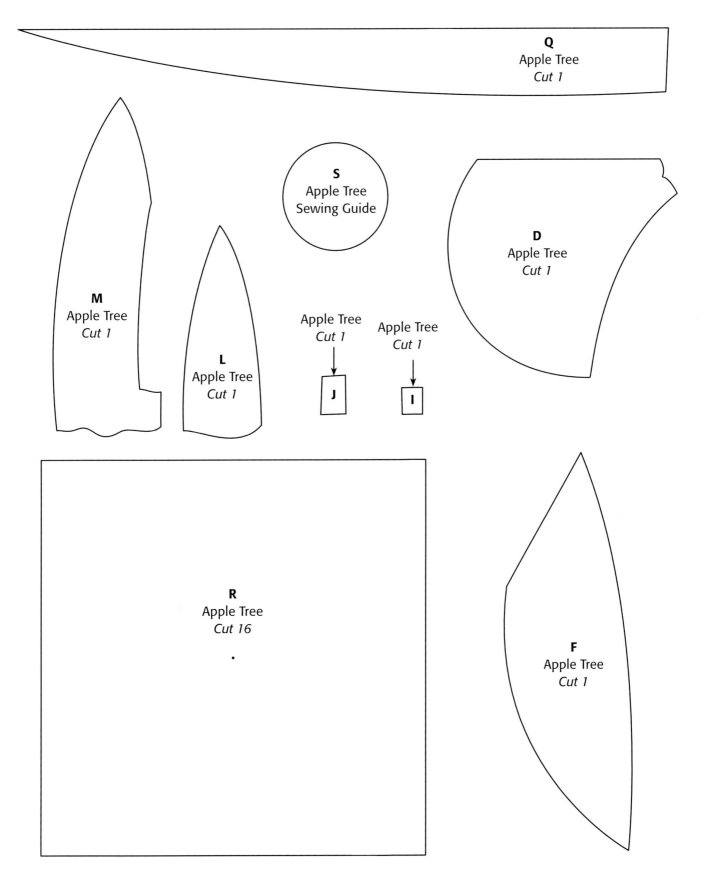

**Q**
Apple Tree
*Cut 1*

**S**
Apple Tree
Sewing Guide

**D**
Apple Tree
*Cut 1*

**M**
Apple Tree
*Cut 1*

**L**
Apple Tree
*Cut 1*

Apple Tree
*Cut 1*

Apple Tree
*Cut 1*

**J**

**I**

**R**
Apple Tree
*Cut 16*

**F**
Apple Tree
*Cut 1*

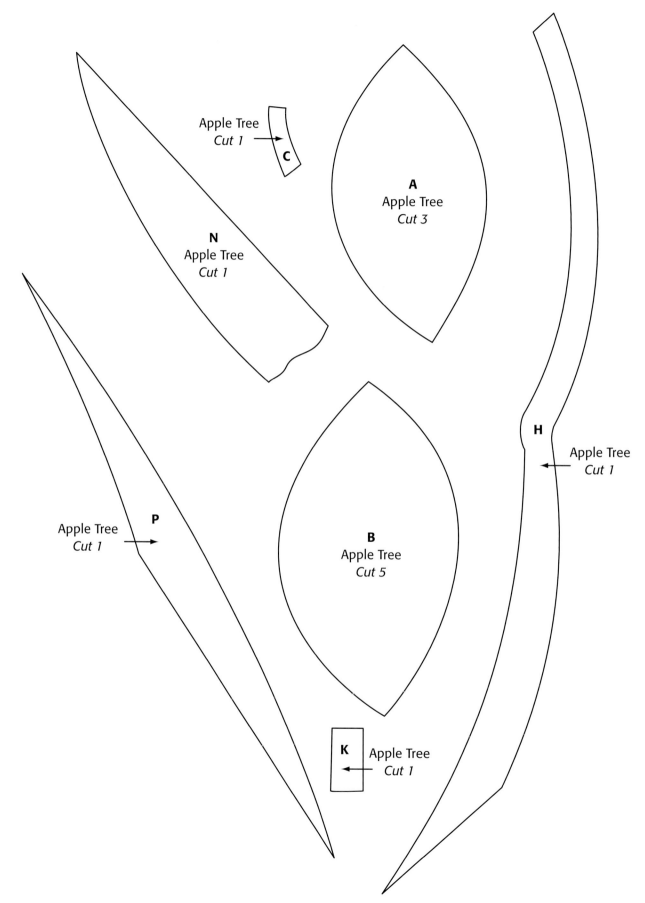

Apple Tree
*Cut 1*

**C**

**N**
Apple Tree
*Cut 1*

**A**
Apple Tree
*Cut 3*

**H**
Apple Tree
*Cut 1*

Apple Tree
*Cut 1*

**P**

**B**
Apple Tree
*Cut 5*

**K** Apple Tree
*Cut 1*

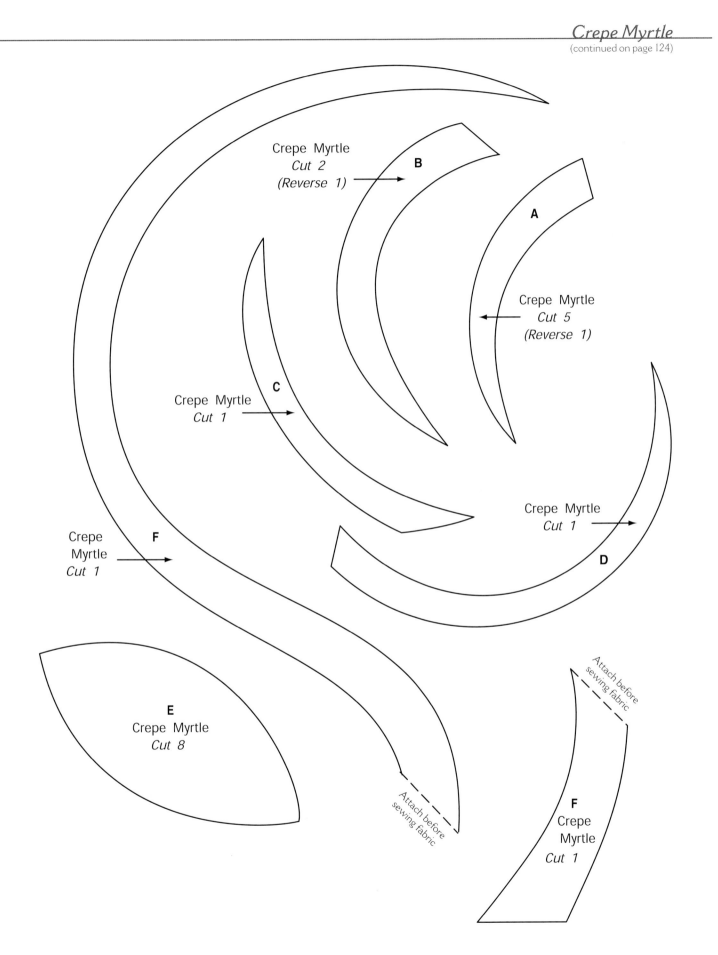

Crepe Myrtle
*Cut 2*
*(Reverse 1)*

B

A

Crepe Myrtle
*Cut 5*
*(Reverse 1)*

Crepe Myrtle
*Cut 1*

C

Crepe Myrtle
*Cut 1*

Crepe
Myrtle
*Cut 1*

F

D

Attach before
sewing fabric

Attach before
sewing fabric

E
Crepe Myrtle
*Cut 8*

F
Crepe
Myrtle
*Cut 1*

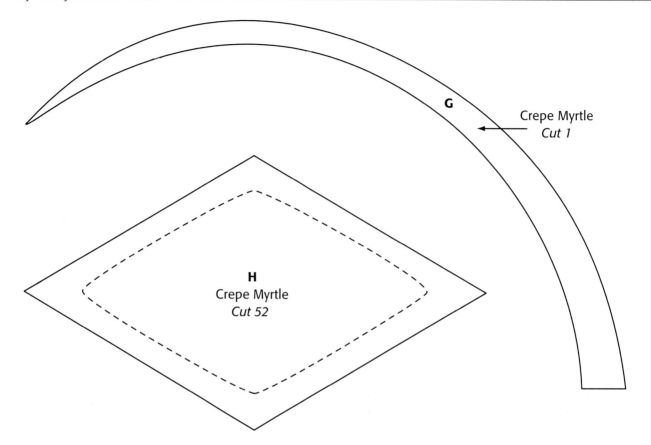

**G**
Crepe Myrtle
*Cut 1*

**H**
Crepe Myrtle
*Cut 52*

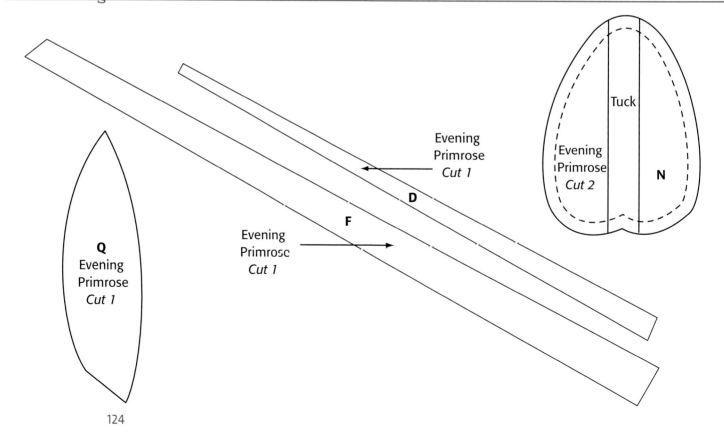

Evening
Primrose
*Cut 1*

**D**

**F**

Evening
Primrose
*Cut 1*

Tuck

Evening
Primrose
*Cut 2*

**N**

**Q**
Evening
Primrose
*Cut 1*

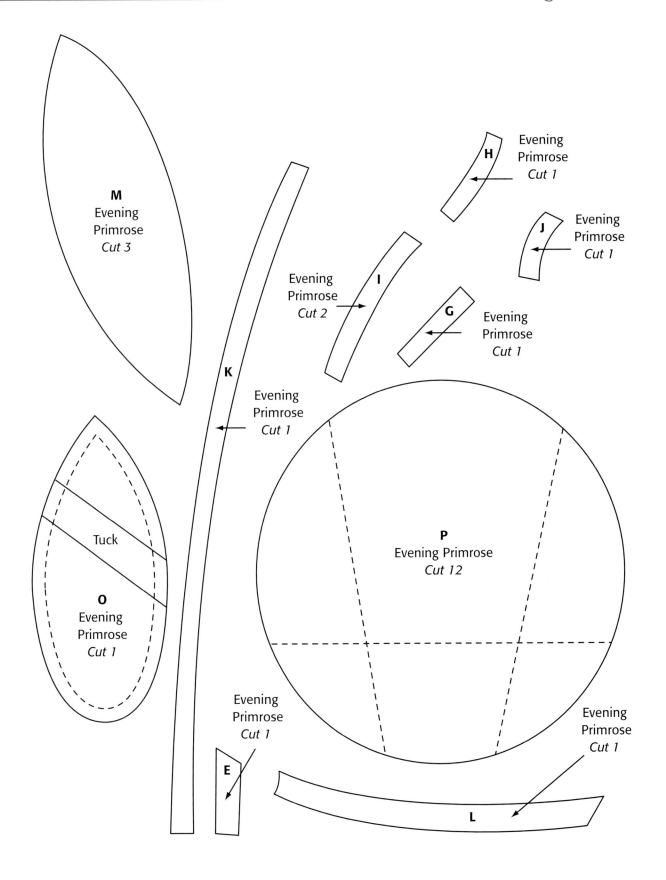

M
Evening
Primrose
*Cut 3*

H
Evening
Primrose
*Cut 1*

J
Evening
Primrose
*Cut 1*

I
Evening
Primrose
*Cut 2*

G
Evening
Primrose
*Cut 1*

K
Evening
Primrose
*Cut 1*

Tuck

O
Evening
Primrose
*Cut 1*

P
Evening Primrose
*Cut 12*

E
Evening
Primrose
*Cut 1*

L
Evening
Primrose
*Cut 1*

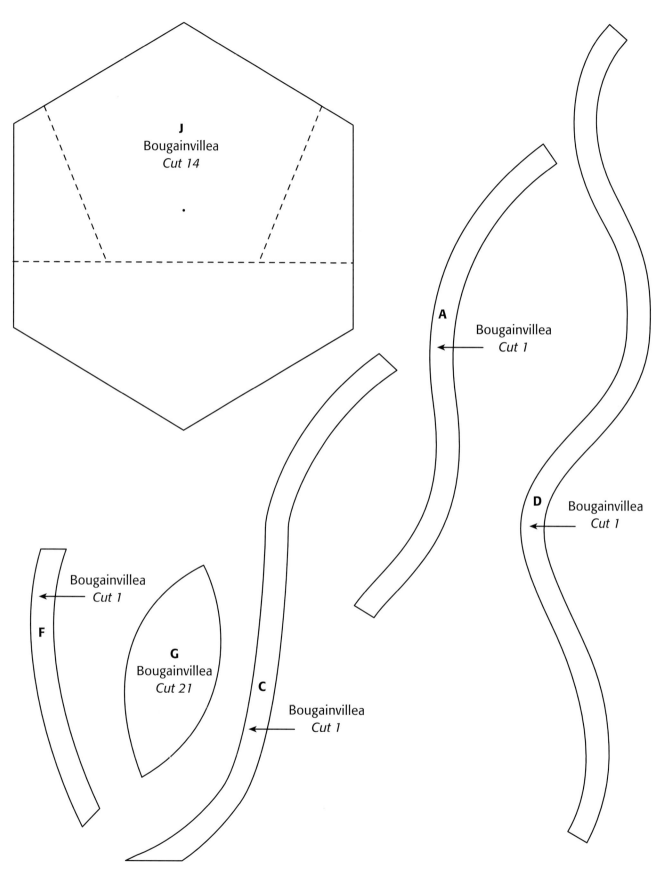

**J**
Bougainvillea
*Cut 14*

**A**
Bougainvillea
*Cut 1*

**D**
Bougainvillea
*Cut 1*

Bougainvillea
*Cut 1*

**F**

**G**
Bougainvillea
*Cut 21*

**C**

Bougainvillea
*Cut 1*

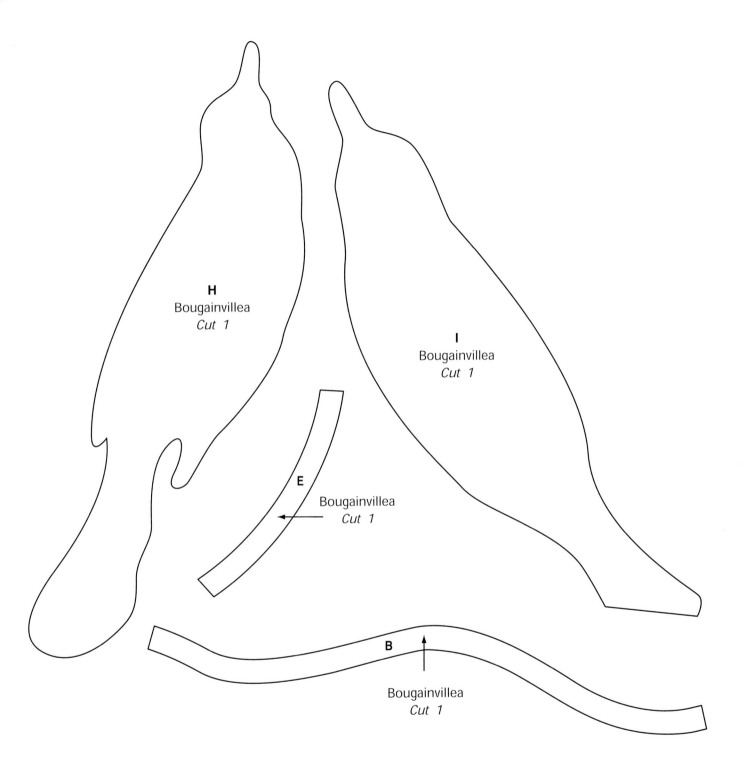

**H**
Bougainvillea
*Cut 1*

**I**
Bougainvillea
*Cut 1*

**E**
Bougainvillea
*Cut 1*

**B**
Bougainvillea
*Cut 1*

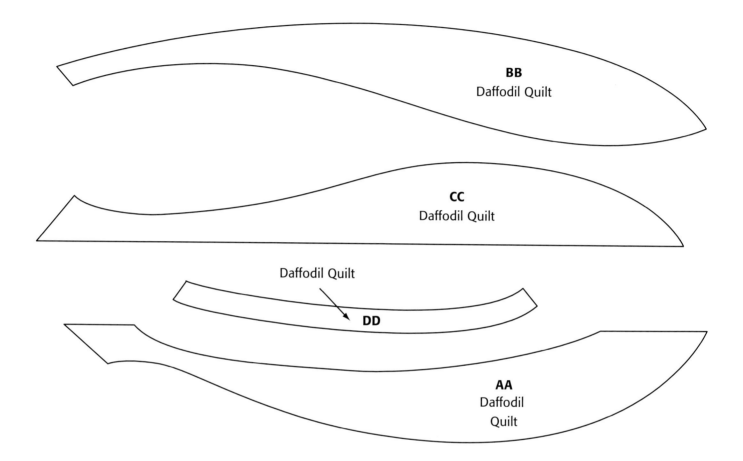

**BB**
Daffodil Quilt

**CC**
Daffodil Quilt

Daffodil Quilt

**DD**

**AA**
Daffodil
Quilt

(continued on page 130)

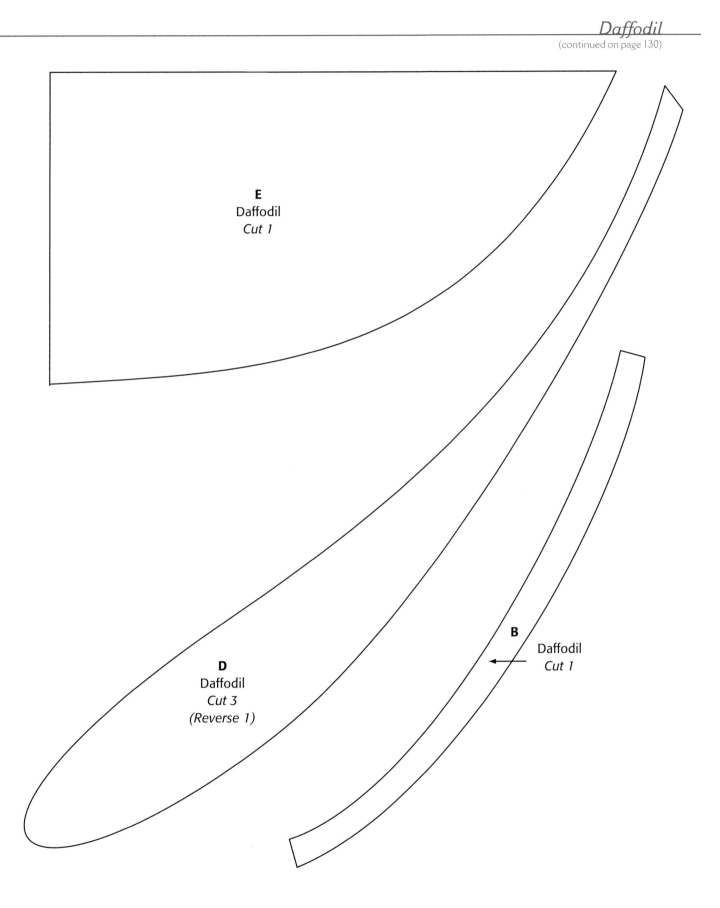

**E**
Daffodil
*Cut 1*

**D**
Daffodil
*Cut 3*
*(Reverse 1)*

**B**
Daffodil
*Cut 1*

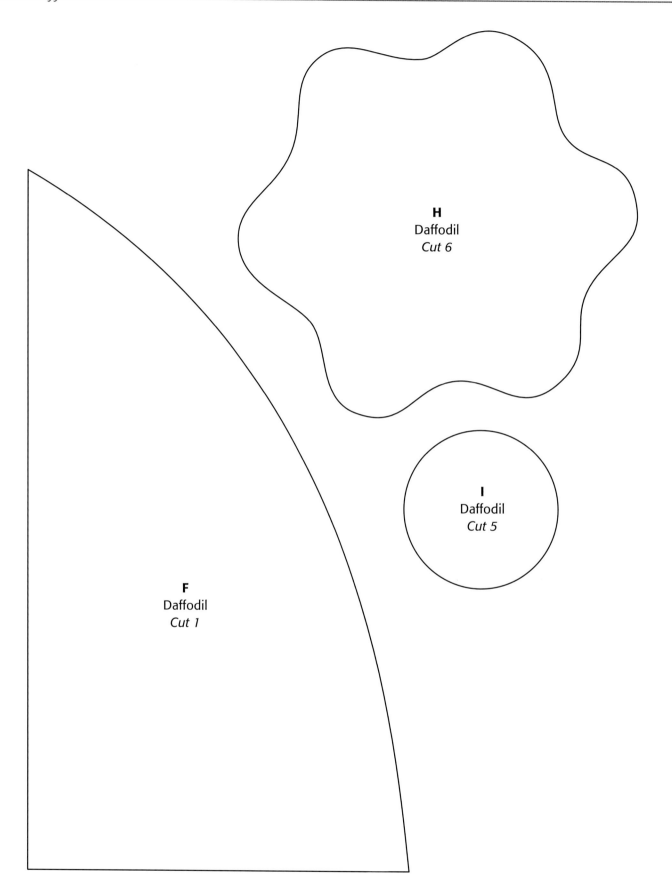

**H**
Daffodil
*Cut 6*

**I**
Daffodil
*Cut 5*

**F**
Daffodil
*Cut 1*

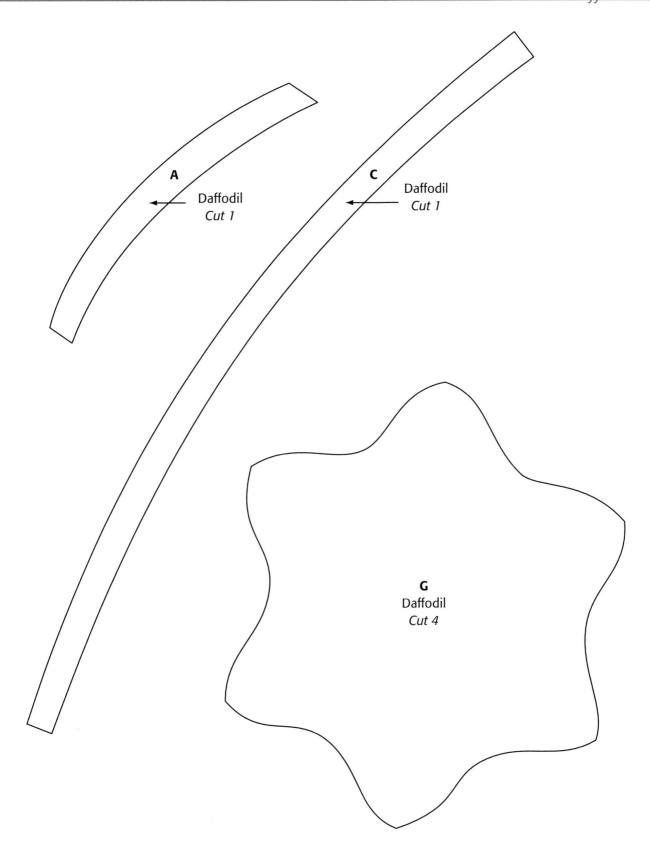

**A**

Daffodil
*Cut 1*

**C**

Daffodil
*Cut 1*

**G**
Daffodil
*Cut 4*

# Lesson Plans

## Supply List

Appliqué needles
Thread
Straight pins
Paper and fabric scissors
Tracing paper
Ruler
Pencil
Colored pencils
Thimble
Fabric marker
White drawing paper
Notebook
Background fabric
Fabric for quilt top
Border fabric
Batting
Backing fabric

## Suggestions for a One-Day Workshop

*Making a Simple Block: Orchid*
*(For Beginning and Intermediate Quilters)*

During this sample lesson, students will make one of the easier blocks
featured in *Fantasies and Flowers*. The process includes learning to work with
templates, learning and practicing a precise method of hand appliqué, and
looking at colors and fabrics in a new way. It also introduces the student to
fabric folding (origami) for three-dimensional effects.

## First Hour

Give each student one or more photocopies of the layout diagram for *Orchid* (page 5). Discuss color selection and placement in the block: contrast of light and dark colors, texture, movement, and use of bold fabric and large design. Instruct students to experiment with color by coloring their photocopies, and then to make their final choices on colors they will use. If you have time, give students some fabric scraps to practice folding fabric to create new shapes.

## Second Hour

Students select background fabric and cut out the background square, following the lengthwise grain or the print of the fabric pattern. Students trace the template pattern pieces on pages 78 to 80 onto white paper. Have them label and cut out each one. Remind students that the pattern pieces do not include seam allowances. Discuss any changes students may want to make to Kumiko's layout of *Orchid*, and help them make any new templates they need. Following the layout diagram on page 5, students lightly draw the outlines of the pattern onto the background fabric using a pencil or fabric marker.

## Third Hour

After discussing the type of fabric to be used for the projects, students select the fabrics that they will need to match their color sketches as closely as possible. They cut all the fabric pieces using the templates, following the lengthwise grain or the print of the fabric patterns. To complete the background square, students pin and appliqué the stems following the instructions on page 5. Have them double-check, using the pattern pieces, that each sewn fabric piece is the right size before going on to the next piece.

## Fourth and Fifth Hours

Students make the flowers following the instructions on page 5. Have students practice the origami folds on scrap fabric before making their flowers. Advise the students to make one complete flower first before starting on the others so that they have a model to follow. Students sew the completed flowers in position onto the background square.

## Sixth Hour

To complete a single block, students join the top, batting, and quilt backing with basting stitches. Show them how to quilt following the seam lines or following a design they select.

# Suggestions for an Extended Classroom Schedule

## Making a More Complex Design: Bleeding Heart Quilt or Block (For Intermediate and Advanced Quilters)

These are ideas to be incorporated into a course for teaching experienced quilters how to refine their appliqué skills and to gain further confidence in using fabric folding to create three-dimensional designs. The course is based on a design that includes many curved seams. More difficult than straight seams, these offer more design possibilities. It also includes suggestions for those who wish to encourage students to create their own three-dimensional designs. Feel free to use these ideas along with your own teaching experience to modify the course as you wish.

Using the *Bleeding Heart* design on page 34, begin by instructing students to make the block following the directions on page 35 and the procedure outlined in the previous class outline. Students may make and finish just one block or the full quilt.

Demonstrate the appliqué technique used in this design. You may also wish to demonstrate other techniques for piecing curved seams and other forms of appliqué.

Discuss the use of color in the project. Have students experiment with different colors and see how the image changes. Try different colors for the background square and the quilt borders, too.

To encourage creativity, demonstrate how new flower designs can be drawn. Students who have completed the *Bleeding Heart* block may wish to progress toward creating their own flower designs. Instruct students to make freehand drawings for a new *Bleeding Heart* block, moving the stems and flowers around the block to create an entirely different image. Use colored pencils to experiment with different colors.

Students who have created new designs can form small groups and share their ideas. Conduct an open discussion about the pros and cons of each design.